LC   Hoskins, Robert L.
2781
.H67   Black administrators
          in higher education

DATE			
APR 2 3 '91			

BLACK ADMINISTRATORS
IN HIGHER EDUCATION

BLACK ADMINISTRATORS IN HIGHER EDUCATION
Conditions and Perceptions

Robert L. Hoskins

 PRAEGER PUBLISHERS
Praeger Special Studies

New York • London • Sydney • Toronto

Library of Congress Cataloging in Publication Data

Hoskins, Robert L
    Black administrators in higher education.

    Bibliography: p.
    1. Afro-American universities and colleges--United
States--Administration. I. Title.
LC2781.H67   378.1'1'0973   78-19740
ISBN 0-03-046611-3

PRAEGER PUBLISHERS
PRAEGER SPECIAL STUDIES
383 Madison Avenue, New York, N.Y. 10017, U.S.A.

Published in the United States of America in 1978
by Praeger Publishers,
A Division of Holt, Rinehart and Winston, CBS, Inc.

89   038   987654321

© 1978 by Robert L. Hoskins

Printed in the United States of America

PREFACE

In the United States today, as in the past, educational attainment is viewed by most people as the "ticket" to success and prosperity, as well as a requirement for dealing successfully with the technologies and complexities of everyday living. Many occupations and professions attempt to upgrade themselves by requiring yet higher and higher levels of education before one can enter those occupations that are considered more desirable. Whether or not schooling and educational attainment are important variables in the equation for social and economic success and prosperity is still being debated. However, today there are millions of students of all ages enrolled in our institutions of higher education, and among these millions are hundreds of thousands of black American students (U.S. Bureau of Census estimates 948,000 blacks were enrolled in higher education in 1975). To these black students the legacy of noneducational attainment has been pointed out as the most pervasive barrier to what has been, and still remains, the elusive mainstream of American life. Therefore, as a result of an awakening of black citizenry and the newly found opportunities to pursue higher education provided by recent federal legislation and federal aids to education, there has been a marked increase in the number of black students enrolled in higher education over the past 15 years.

There exists the dilemma that there are hundreds of thousands of black students pursuing higher education but a dearth of black faculty and staff in higher education. Consequently, the ratio of black faculty and staff in higher education to the number of black students is out of proportion on a national basis. Most black faculty and staff in higher education are concentrated in the approximately 120 black colleges and universities. The majority of black faculty and staff outside predominantly black higher institutions are primarily in urban colleges and universities.

While the number of black faculty and staff is small, black administrators are differentially an even smaller population in higher education. Many of the black administrators outside the traditional black colleges and universities only recently have gotten the call to join the faculties and staffs of majority higher institutions. Also, most black administrators recently employed at majority institutions are said to have been placed in newly created temporary positions that carry the connotation of "window dressers" or "tokens" because of the lack of authority and power in these positions to act in situations other than those related to minority affairs.

Recent trends in higher education indicate that with the lessening of campus unrest and volatile student demands, fewer blacks are being hired into the ranks of majority institutions and even fewer are being given tenure and/or promotions. Among already established and aspiring black academicians, there are those who would seek careers in higher educational administration. Therefore, it becomes important to explore the variables considered most important to the success and longevity of black administrators, and to determine the differences between working in a black institution of higher education and in a white institution of higher education.

As a result of these concerns, a national survey was conducted during 1976-77. Working out of the University of Wisconsin-Milwaukee's School of Medicine, Office of Research. Directed by Dr. Adrian Chan, the nation's land-grant institutions of higher education were surveyed by the author and a population of 457 black administrators was determined. This population was then separated into two groups for comparison by chi-square analyses on 52 variables related to background variables and selected perceptions of black administrators working at predominantly black land-grant institutions as compared to black administrators working at predominantly white land-grant institutions. The results of the study make up the majority of this book.

CONTENTS

Chapter

Chapter

LIST OF TABLES

1

INTRODUCTION

Now that college campuses are no longer embroiled in turmoil and violent conflict, many of the more recently acquired black scholars on campus in teaching positions and the few that are in administration at the ivory tower institutions of higher education find their positions tenuous at best. Many of these individuals must surely be wondering why previously amicable relationships are deteriorating. Tenure and promotions are not coming, and those same people in "Old Main," who were so glad to welcome aboard the black experts only a few years ago, seem to have adopted the attitude that "as volatile seas calm, black academicians should move on." In many cases, the black on the majority campus is now being made very uncomfortable and often treated contemptuously in the hope that he will go away, now that he has put out the fires. However, there are many variables to be explored in assessing the condition of black administrators at white colleges and universities and how these conditions compare to those of black administrators at black colleges and universities.

Unfortunately, very little investigation has been done relative to black administrators in higher education. Therefore, the task of finding and identifying black administrators at white colleges and universities is difficult at best. Once the black administrator has been located, then the question becomes: What are his perceptions concerning the conditions surrounding his employment and how does he differ from a black administrator at a black school? It should be readily understood that black administrators will differ in their individual situations, just as there are certain to be differences in atmospheres from one campus to the next. However, there are many interests generated around such variables as differences in background characteristics between black administrators at black and white institutions.

What methods, if not sheer panic recruitment efforts, were used in the selection process? Do the selection processes differ between black and white institutions when black administrators are being chosen? A formidable question is: Do the professional characteristics of black administrators at black institutions differ from those of black administrators at white institutions?

Many black students and others have viewed the black administrator on the white campus as a "token"—often without having had meaningful contact or dialogue with the individual. It must, of course, be suspected that many "token" positions were created when black students proliferated white campuses starting in the 1960s.

The recent past has shown a tendency for majority higher institutions to place newly arrived black scholars in positions that tend to deal with black and other minority student concerns only—admissions offices, financial aids, student centers, minority affairs, special assistants to the chancellor or president, and black studies programs. Thus, to many militants and others, black administrators' power and decision-making authority were viewed as relegated to opinions given in private conferences with his/her superiors to advise on how to handle some minority student flare-up or to act as intermediary to settle minority student grievances. Therefore, it is interesting to determine if the opinions and perceptions about their employment differ greatly between black administrators at black and white higher institutions.

Nonblack administrators in most instances have traditionally risen from the ranks of the faculty to dean and vice-president and have often culminated their ascent with the presidency of an institution. Most black faculty and administrators, however, have only recently been recruited to majority campuses in the wake of rapidly expanded minority student populations. Therefore, most black scholars cannot climb the administrative ladder in the same order as do their white counterparts.

The first recorded Ph.D. awarded to a black person in the United States dates back to Edward Bouchet in 1876 (Ph.D. in physics, Yale University). The next two blacks awarded the degree were J. W. E. Bowen in 1887 (Ph.D. in religion, Boston University) and Alfred O. Coffin in 1889 (Ph.D. in biological science, Illinois Wesleyan University).[1] At present, there is no accurate account of the number of black persons with Ph.D.s or of how many black Ph.D.s live in the United States. Estimates range from 1,500 to about 3,000[2,3] (Transaction 1970; Moore and Wagstaff 1974). Whatever figure is accepted, it is obvious that there is a severe shortage of blacks who hold the doctorate.

The Ph.D. is not necessarily the only prerequisite to becoming a higher educational administrator, as there are many administators, both black and white, who do not hold an earned doctorate. However, black administrators in the higher rank positions at major institutions are more likely to have earned doctorates.

It might be concluded that the task of attracting blacks into higher educational administration is difficult. Certainly, many majority institutions voice that opinion as explanation for their inability to attract black academicians when answering questions about affirmative action and integration. Nonetheless, it is assumed that black scholars can be attracted to higher educational administration, black scholars have not priced themselves out of the academic marketplace, and major institutions have failed in their efforts to locate and hire black Ph.D.s, many of whom work in federal service because of their inability to find positions in higher education. Therefore, the thrust of this study was to explore those variables—promotion and career factors, black-white relations, and task stereotyping after recruitment—considered most pertinent to the recruitment and retention of black professionals in higher educational administration.

Some difficulties resulted from a scarcity of black administrators outside the predominantly black colleges and universities. Also, it is a difficult task to locate black administrators who work at white institutions. To facilitate a reasonable time and cost and to ensure a population of black administrators who work at white institutions of higher education, only land-grant institutions of higher education were sampled. By using land-grant colleges and universities throughout the United States and its territories and possessions, a representative sample of black administrators who work at black and white higher institutions was obtained to the extent that land-grant colleges and universities are representative of black and white public higher institutions, comparisons of selected criteria relative to background characteristics and professional perceptions of black administrators who work at those black and white institutions of higher education have been provided.

If this study had been designed to sample administrators on a nationwide basis, a considerable capital outlay and a very large staff and from two to three years time would have been required. Only one year was required to gather the information from the land-grant institutions.

The population of black administrators that was drawn from land-grant colleges and universities consisted of all black administrators with the title of assistant dean or higher title or equivalent faculty or staff titles. The institutions from which the population of black administrators was drawn consisted of all of the 72 land-grant institutions, with the exception of six that would not participate. Their campuses are found in all of the 50 United States, Guam, Puerto Rico, the Virgin Islands, and the District of Columbia. Seventeen of the land-grant institutions are predominantly black. Both black and white institutions range in size from small, through medium, to large, and are found in small towns in rural areas, in medium-sized cities, and in the largest cities and metropolitan areas. Many of these institutions have multiple campuses. However, the white institutions surveyed have few blacks on their faculties and in their administrations. In fact, some of these institutions have no blacks on their faculties and administrative staffs.

While land-grant institutions represent less than 4 percent of the nation's colleges and universities, they enroll over 25 percent of the nation's college students. They also grant over 25 percent of all degree awarded in the United States.

The 457 black administrators who were located were asked to respond to a questionnaire that solicited information relative to demographic data, methods of recruitment and/or selection by which they obtained their present administrative position, professional characteristics, and their attitudes and opinions toward their present employment.

Hypotheses were formulated relative to the anticipated differences between black administrators who work at black higher institutions and black administrators who work at white higher institutions. The hypotheses are:

1. No differences exist in the background characteristics of black administrators who work at black and white land-grant institutions of higher education.
2. No differences exist in the methods of recruitment and/or selection of black administrators who work at black and white land-grant institutions of higher education.
3. No differences exist in the professional characteristics of black administrators who work at black and white land-grant institutions of higher education.
4. No differences exist in the opinions and perceptions toward employment of black administrators who work at black and white land-grant institutions of higher education.

Statistical analyses of the data were applied as described in Chapter 3. Chapters 4 through 7 present the findings of the study, followed by the conclusions and recommendations in Chapter 8. Chapter 2 presents others' thoughts on the subject.

NOTES

1. Harry Washington Green, Holders of Doctorates Among American Negroes (Newton, Mass.: Crofton, 1974).

2. "Black Ph.D.s: A Survey of Black American Doctorates," Transaction 7 (May 1970): 14.

3. William Moore, Jr., and Lonnie H. Wagstaff, Black Educators in White Colleges (San Francisco: Jossey-Bass, 1974).

2

REVIEW OF THE LITERATURE

Roald F. Campbell[1] has stated that when types of administrators are compared at the managerial level the elements seem to be similar for educational, industrial, civil, hospital, and business administrations. However, at the technical and institutional levels, educational administration appears to differ dramatically from other forms of administrations. Educational administration has much more public visibility and sensitivity at the institutional level than other types. Education administrators are said to rely much less on standard operating procedures than administrators in industry. Therefore, they are affected by the need for superior intelligence, professional values, and a high degree of articulation.

Of more importance is the fact that educational institutions are not in business for profit and are much more visible publicly than other institutions, with not one but many publics. These publics often differ considerably in their perspectives about the task and direction of education.

Campbell's findings suggest that only in recent years have educators begun to take a serious look at higher educational administration and its relationship to the broader society and the implications of those relationships to administrative behavior. This accentuates further the unique character of educational administration and the need for more research relative to its peculiar characteristics. If educational administration is unique in the field of administration in general, then one could infer that black educational administrators are in a unique position within higher educational administration.

It would appear that black administrators are desperately needed but are not being developed at a rate consistent with the need. Roosevelt Johnson[2] has noted that traditionally white scholars have followed a regular ascension pattern to become college administrators.

Black scholars, however, due to their scarcity outside the traditional black colleges until most recently, have not been able to follow a
regular ascension pattern to college administration.

Black administrators are usually hired into impotent administrative positions. They lack power and authority to make administrative decisions in areas other than black studies and minority
affairs, primarily because no thought was given to the possibility of
black administrators being on white campuses prior to the mid-1960s.
Therefore, until recently, blacks have not had the chance to serve in
administrative positions outside the predominantly black institutions.

Johnson concluded that there should be an institute for black
college administrators, that white colleges should hire black administrators into decision-making positions, and that black administrators' positions should not be diminished when the era of overt black
student protest and demands for government affirmative action
subsides.

Blacks who do not hold the Ph.D. should also be considered
for other administrative positions in higher education commensurate
with their training. However, Johnson stresses that blacks who suc-
ceed in higher education should not forget their origin or let a sub-
surface self-hate syndrome impair their sense of responsibility to
other blacks.

A survey of black American doctorates was conducted by the
Offices of Special Projects at the Ford Foundation in 1970, primarily
as the result of black students demanding relevant programs of
studies.[3] The findings included the following: There are few young
black Ph.D.s; only 9.4 percent of them are under 34 years of age
and most (55.9 percent) are 45 or older. The majority of black
Ph.D.s received their undergraduate training at black colleges. The
degree came hard; more than 70 percent of the black Ph.D.s took 10
years or more after finishing college, 21.4 percent took more than
20 years. There is no reservoir of black Ph.D.s currently working
outside of academia.* Of those surveyed, 85.4 percent already work
in higher education, 5.3 percent are employed by government agencies,

---

*The contention of the Office of Special Projects at the Ford
Foundation that there is no reservoir of black Ph.D.s currently working outside academia has been repudiated by William Moore and Lonnie Wagstaff (1974). They thus state "other blacks who earned the
Ph.D. were forced into taking positions with the Federal Government.
The salaries were higher, but most of them never rose above the
lower grade levels" (p. 46).

and 4.8 percent work for private agencies such as the NAACP and
the National Urban League. The situation is not improving: surveys
for 1964 through 1968 showed that only 0.8 percent of the Ph.D.s
awarded went to black candidates. The Ford Foundation believes that
the number would have increased 20 percent by 1973. However, with
that increase, blacks would only have increased overall from 1 to 2
percent of the national total of Ph.D.s.

Jacquelyne J. Jackson[4] has repudiated some of the Ford Foundation's findings. According to Jackson, the mailed questionnaire
contained no question or item relating to the difficulty of obtaining the
Ph.D., referring to the statement that "the degree came hard to those
who have it; more than 70 percent of black Ph.D.s took ten years or
more after finishing college to win the degree; and for 21.4 percent
the process took more than 20 years." She also noted that the analysis
of data done by the Office of Special Projects was based upon the number of years that lapsed between the awarding of one's bachelor degree and the awarding of one's doctoral degree. A more valid interpretation would be that black Ph.D.s in the subject group had a discontinuous educational process.

Jackson concluded the following: Financial support has been
very minimal for black Ph.D. students until recently. Outside of the
black institutions there has been no demand for black Ph.D.s until
very recently. More should be done to ensure opportunities for black
Ph.D.s once they have obtained the degree (that is, a variety of higher level positions with proper financial compensation). Above all,
Jackson feels, black Ph.D.s should not be considered only for positions in black studies programs.

Another study of national scope by Harold M. Rose,[5] relative
to the topic of blacks in higher education, has revealed the following:
There have been few studies that have concentrated upon black Ph.D.s
in the marketplace; many blacks prefer to remain in the closed system of the South where they might help to raise the level of black education; institutions of higher education have discriminated against
blacks in hiring faculty; many administrators are beginning to show
concern about the lack of blacks among their ranks; only a few highly
regarded institutions of higher education have a history of hiring black
educators, and the total number hired is small; only 139 black academicians had served on faculties outside the South during the 1940s—
only 54 of those had been employed on a continuous basis and only 3
of the 54 had been employed prior to 1940; only 65 blacks were employed in higher education outside the South in 1960; most blacks were
employed by urban universities because of the growing numbers of
black students; blacks in the sciences were most sought after by
academia; blacks who obtained undergraduate degrees at southern
black colleges were less likely to be found on college faculties in the

North. Rose's conclusion was that the nation's colleges and universities have not taken a position of leadership in the expansion of employment opportunities for black educators.

Compounding the dilemma of the lack of black Ph.D.s and
black college administrators, black student protests for more relevant
offerings during the mid-1960s caused white higher institutions to re-
act in such a way as to create what Eddie W. Morris[6] and others have
called the "brain drain," that is, black scholars being lured away
from black colleges and universities by white institutions.

In the Morris study, 50 black colleges of 73 contacted responded
to a questionnaire sent to selected black colleges listed in the direc-
tory of the National Association of College Deans and Registrars.
These were found to be representative of black colleges (with the exception of junior colleges). Thirty-three of the 50 colleges said that
they had lost valuable black faculty to white colleges, government,
and industry. Over half of the black colleges stated that they found
the lost faculty hard to replace with faculty of equal ability. Thirty-
eight of the 50 colleges found it very difficult to recruit black faculty.
It was found that competent white faculty was easier to recruit. Half
of the black colleges also said that they could not pay salaries asked
by black scholars—white institutions paid much more.

Morris concluded that black professors were being sought because of pressure from government and from campus militants; most
white colleges want to employ black scholars in newly established
minority programs; boards of white institutions want their institutions
to demonstrate that they believe in equal opportunity and integration;
black scholars tend to believe that they are furthering the process of
integration and equal opportunity; and black scholars want better
facilities within which to teach and do research and want the possibility of leave-time.

Morris recommends that more financial aid be given to black
colleges to put them on a par with white colleges. There should be a
sharing of faculty for certain periods of time. Also, more blacks
must be graduated from doctoral programs. Most importantly, black
scholars must reaffirm their commitment to minority education and
progress and not lose contact and sympathy for less fortunate blacks.

Agreement with the Morris research is found in a survey conducted for the U.S. Department of Health, Education, and Welfare.[7]
The survey showed that there are striking differences between faculty
employed by institutions of higher education attended by white students
and those attended predominantly by black students. For example,
faculty at black colleges have a higher proportion of women, a minority of earned doctorates (28 percent), lower academic rank, and lower salaries. Also, faculty in black colleges teach mostly undergraduates. Faculty at white colleges teach more sciences (33 percent) as

compared to black colleges (18 percent). Conversely, 36 percent of
black college faculty teach education compared to 21 percent of white
college faculty.

Earl Huyck also found that there were no Ph.D.s conferred by
black colleges and universities between 1947 and 1954 and that no
more than four Ph.D.s were granted by black colleges and universities between 1954 and 1964. At that time, black Ph.D.s were being
produced nationally at the rate of four per year, and most of those
were being employed by black colleges.

It is important to assess the attitudes of black scholars toward
black colleges and universities. The willingness of black professors
in predominantly white institutions to teach and administer at black
colleges and to encourage others to attend these schools must be
examined. Experiences of the respondents in black institutions must
also be examined.

In research conducted by David M. Rafky,[8] in 1969, a precoded
questionnaire was mailed to 699 black faculty members in predominantly white colleges and universities with more than 300 students
outside the South. Seventy-nine percent (554) responded. Multivari-
ate procedures were used to examine a series of independent variables
against three dependent variables: previous teaching experience in
black colleges, willingness to encourage others to attend a black college, and willingness to teach in a black college. The findings related
to the three dependent variables are as follows:

Blacks who have taught in black colleges tend to hold doctorates
earned from high-quality universities and have published one or more
books or articles. Usually, they taught humanities, languages, and/
or education. They use the less militant label "Negro" instead of
"black" and are now employed in state-supported high-quality white
schools. Age is the most important variable relative to previous
teaching experience in black colleges (most having had the experience
are 50 and older). Upper socioeconomic status blacks who graduated
from black colleges are more likely to teach at black colleges than
lower socioeconomic status blacks who graduated from black colleges.
Blacks who spent their first 18 years of life in the South and graduated from a black college are most likely to have taught in a black
college. Those who were raised in the South and attended a white
college are less likely to have taught in a black institution.

Forty-two percent of the respondents would not recommend
black institutions because these schools allegedly do not prepare students for living in an integrated society and because of the reputed
low quality of black institutions of higher education. However, 50
percent do recommend black colleges. Of this number, most feel
that there are very positive social and psychological benefits. Blacks
who have taught in black colleges are more likely to encourage

attending them. In general, the younger respondents were most likely to recommend black colleges.

Eighty-seven percent of the respondents indicated that they
would teach in black colleges, even though many are nearing retirement and many must complete previous commitments.

Rafky concluded that the brain drain could be abated. Also,
he concluded, many blacks would teach in black colleges if they were
sought out and asked.

Many black Ph.D.s want to make a contribution to black institutions of higher education, but at the same time are ambivalent because of the inducements offered by the large majority universities
and foundations of better working conditions and higher salaries.
Wayman B. Shiver, Jr.,[9] has stated that many black educators who
have never made decent salaries are being offered double their present
salaries to join the faculties of major institutions. Black colleges
cannot offer competitive salaries. Too often, black college presidents
are only able to offer titles and promises of better things when times
are better. In order to make a reasonable salary in most black colleges, the black professors have to wear many hats: administer
projects, teach, consult, and make many speeches. Shiver also
states that black professors who are hired by major white institutions
appear to meet the needs of black students, whom they are ostensibly
hired to serve.

A national assessment of blacks in academia has been provided
recently by Kent G. Mommsen.[10] He collected survey data through
a national sample of black Ph.D.s in the United States in 1970. Questionnaires were sent to 2,305 names believed to be black Ph.D.s.
There were 1,383 responses (52 percent); 317 others were undeliver-
able and 281 were not in the population.

The findings were that there is no exact way to determine the
number of black Ph.D.s in the United States. Most blacks receive
their doctorates from large, prestigious, predominantly white institutions. More than 79 percent of black Ph.D.s work in predominantly
black institutions. There is, however, much demand for black Ph.D.s.
Many offers are received by black scholars (four per year on the average). These scholars are asking a high price before considering a
move. However, the median salary of black Ph.D.s is slightly below
that of whites on a national average. Blacks are mobile and will consider moving to other positions. The conclusion reached by Mommsen
is that, based upon supply and demand, blacks have not priced themselves out of the academic marketplace.

An assessment of the situation of black scholars who have been
recently hired for administrative positions at white colleges indicates
that they are not given regular positions but are usually given "special"
positions that signify impermanence. There is, says Bennie L. Wiley,[11]

a great need for blacks to be hired into regular established university positions because nearly all blacks in university administration are in newly created positions that have little power or authority. Wiley also states that most administrative positions open to blacks are in the area of human relations. He further notes that black administrators are expected to solve all racial problems and conflicts, and are expected to head impotent committees to find and hire other black professionals. Thus, Wiley concludes that black administrators are usually hired to absorb criticism aimed at the college or university when something goes wrong in the area of race relations, affirmative action, or integration. Therefore, black educators are becoming reluctant to fill token administrative positions. If changes do not occur, higher educational administration will become more segregated.

At the First National Congress of Black Professionals in Higher Education at the University of Texas-Austin (April 5-7, 1972), Bernard C. Watson[12] stated that the black administrator is important to both black and white institutions. The supply of black administrators is very limited because of the historic lack of opportunity for both training and placement. Also, the black administrator must possess skills to cope with special problems in addition to the normal administrative duties. There are also demands growing out of his/her blackness.

Watson further said that "there must be conceptualization and implementation of valid theoretical and practical approaches for the training, education and development of black administrators. There must be a short and long-range recruitment effort to increase the supply of black administrators."[13] Watson concluded that there should be internships for prospective black administrators at both black and white institutions. Also, people with backgrounds in business and industry can successfully work in college administration and should be given consideration.

The implications, as Watson sees them, are that black college administrators must come to the forefront in the battle to improve black existence through education. Honest black history must be stressed and black educators must put a stop to irrational rhetoric by uninformed radicals.

Watson proposed that a National Foundation for Higher Education be established and that there be a black codirector. Predominantly white institutions with large black enrollments should employ at least one black policy-making administrator. Also, black institutions should start more mutual cooperative programs and try to increase the number of black students and professionals in higher educational administration.

In an editorial in Ebony[14] on the Cheek brothers, James Cheek, upon assuming the presidency of strife-torn Howard University, stated that administrations must make way for more responsiveness to demands of black students for more meaningful and up-to-date programs of study. The Cheek brothers also expressed the opinion that black colleges and universities should set up urban university centers in the North, because major white universities do not show genuine concern for the education of blacks.* Also, black students on white campuses are usually there to enhance the universities' position for seeking and getting federal funds.

The conclusions reached by the Cheek brothers are that there still is a great need for the black colleges and universities. Black administrators must take a more futuristic look at education. And there will be a definite need for more black college administrators if black students are to receive meaningful education.

In exploring the attitudes, observations, and opinions among college administrators, Harvey R. HoHouser[15] hypothesized that black administrators would show bureaucratic and professional attitudes somewhat different from those displayed by white administrators in similar occupational positions. He further hypothesized that "black administrators as members of an ethnic sub-culture would be influenced by their 'ethnicity' and would evince interpretations of bureaucratic and professional attitudes which would deviate from normative models of bureaucracy and professionalism."[16]

His findings were that (1) black administrators tended to manifest attitudinal predispositions that were typically congruent with normative prescriptions of bureaucracy and professionalism. Also, this pattern of conformity usually exceeded those displayed by a comparative white sample. (2) Age, current job position, highest academic degree, and prior administrative experience were of extreme significance to the outcome of this study. That is, those administrators who were youngest, had not attained the doctoral degree, and had fewer administrative appointments, and so on, tended to identify more with attitudes of bureaucracy and bureaucratic professionalism. (3) Racial identity was determined to be less significant than age, job experiences, degree level, and present occupational level on affecting attitudes.

---

*James Cheek had been president of Shaw University before assuming the presidency of Howard University. King Cheek, his brother, succeeded him as president of Shaw University.

Commensurate with the HoHouser hypotheses, Christopher
Jencks and David Riesman[17] made a study of Negro colleges, enrollment trends, and future expectations. Their findings were that Negro
colleges tend to stress social rather than intellectual or vocational
ambitions. Most black colleges fail to influence their immediate surrounding area, that is, provide extension services for business and
industry. Most black colleges are located too close to each other.
Many of the black colleges maintain integrated faculties but seldom
have integrated student bodies. Black college presidents are said to
be reluctant to speak of future goals of their colleges in regard to
integration. The intellectual atmosphere of black colleges, stated
Jencks and Riesman, is oppressive, and black college presidents are
dictatorial.

Jencks and Riesman consider black colleges inferior to white
colleges. The 12 best black colleges are said to compare to average
white colleges. They conclude that many black colleges should con-
solidate. Black colleges should develop specialized offerings and
upgrade their academics. Black colleges should develop curricula
that fulfill the needs of black people in their respective localities.
They further state that black colleges should develop more professional schools and also concentrate on solving black-related problems.
Unless these steps are taken, Jencks and Reisman believe, black
colleges and universities will not improve much in the near future,
nor will opportunities for black administrators.

Traditionally, most of the nation's black colleges are in the
South and usually have had ministers as presidents. However, as a
result of interviewing black college presidents, a "new breed" has
evolved, according to Time magazine.[18] In the past, black college
presidents allegedly did not demand much, and as a result their colleges have not compared with the growth rate of white colleges. The
"new breed" of black college presidents are professional educators
and are taking a more realistic approach to the demands of their
presidencies. They are said to be on the road to improving their
colleges, both academically and physically. These new presidents
are said to be more socially militant than their predecessors, and
they are concerned that their colleges begin to provide services to
the surrounding black communities. They are also said to be more
aware of the changing social and political views of black students and
also students' changing academic and social needs.

Most recently, Intellect[19] editorially surmised that the position of blacks in higher education over the past 10 years is still unequal even though improved. Even with supportive legislation, court
decisions, affirmative action, and increased financial aid, blacks
have not been able to break down the barriers that exist in higher
education on the whole. There continue to be barriers to equal educational opportunity.

Intellect further stated that the Office of Civil Rights of the U.S. Department of Health, Education, and Welfare and the U.S. Census Bureau differ in both the statistics reported and collection methods. Unequal educational and employment opportunity is concluded to amount to $8.5 billion in annual losses for black Americans. Therefore, Intellect recommended that federally funded annual higher education general information surveys include racial figures on the enrollment and degrees awarded. Also, research and teaching fellowships for blacks, as well as cost-of-education allowances for institutions, should be greatly expanded.

RESTATEMENT

In reviewing the literature on blacks in higher education generally, and blacks in higher educational administration specifically, this investigator has found that black administrators in higher education are in a unique position of being desperately needed but are not being developed at a rate consistent with the need. One reason for this situation is that while black administrators at black institutions have been able to follow regular ascension patterns to becoming college administrators, the same is not true at major institutions—in part due to a lack of black faculty at most major higher institutions before the 1960s. According to Johnson, black administrators are usually hired into impotent administrative positions because no thought was given to the possibility of blacks having to be in administrative positions on white campuses prior to the mid-1960s. Johnson further states that blacks who do not hold the Ph.D. should also be considered for administrative positions in higher education commensurate with their training. This in fact might well already be true when we consider that the findings of this investigator show that approximately half of the total number of respondents in administrative positions at black and white land-grant institutions hold the Ph.D.

A survey of black American doctorates that was conducted for the Ford Foundation in 1970 concluded in part that more than 70 percent of the black Ph.D.s took 10 years or more after finishing college to earn the doctorate and many blacks took more than 20 years to earn the degree. Jackson repudiated the findings of the Ford Foundation's Office of Special Projects and stated that a more valid interpretation would be that black Ph.D.s in the subject group had a discontinuous educational process. Another finding of the Office of Special Projects was that there is no reservoir of black Ph.D.s currently working outside of academia. This finding is contradictory to the findings of Moore and Wagstaff, who state that many black Ph.D.s were forced into taking positions outside higher education due to lack of opportunity within the field. This contention is further supported

by the findings of Rose. Rose also points out that many black scholars prefer to remain at black higher educational institutions because
of past and present discriminatory hiring practices of major institutions

Morris asserts that there has been a brain drain, as many
black scholars have been lured away from black colleges and universities by white higher institutions. Presently, there does not seem
to be a brain drain. The findings of the investigator support the contention that major institutions are not presently recruiting black land-
grant institutions as actively as in the recent past.

In making an assessment of the attitudes of black scholars toward working in and recommending black colleges and universities,
Rafky found that most black scholars who are not presently working at
black higher institutions would do so if they were asked. However,
many black scholars who have wanted to contribute to the cause of
black education have also been faced with the dilemma of being offered
ideal working conditions and much higher salary by major white institutions. Presently, that condition no longer seems to prevail. The
findings of this investigator's exploration of black administrators
working at black and white land-grant institutions show that many
black scholars are seeking out or returning to black institutions.
Also, there is no significant difference between the salaries of black
administrators working at black and white land-grant institutions.

Shiver has noted that black professors who are hired by major
white institutions appear to meet the needs of white students more
often than they meet the needs of black students, whom they are usually hired to serve. However, this investigator has found that black
administrators at white land-grant institutions show much more active
concern for voluntary involvement with black studies and black students than their counterparts at black land-grant institutions.

Mommsen's national survey of blacks in academia has led
him to believe that there is much demand for black Ph.D.s and most
of them receive on the average four position offers per year. These
scholars are said to be asking a high price before they will consider
moving. Even so, the median salary of black Ph.D.s is slightly below that of white Ph.D.s on a national level.

In assessing the situation of black scholars who more recently
have been hired into the administrations of white colleges, Wiley says
they have voiced that their positions are tenuous and are usually in
the area of human relations where they are expected to solve all racial problems and conflicts. Wiley also says that black administrators
are usually hired to absorb criticism aimed at the college or university in the area of race relations, affirmative action, and other minority concerns.

HoHouser has demonstrated that black administrators' attitudes
and dispositions conform to the norms of all college administrators,

contradicting the previous findings by Jencks and Riesman, which characterized black college administrators at black colleges to be oppressive and dictatorial. The most recent summarization of the situation of blacks in higher education by Intellect is that the position of blacks has not improved over the past 10 years. Even with supportive legislation, court decisions, affirmative action, and increased financial aid, discrimination and lack of opportunity still persist.

NOTES

1. Roald F. Campbell, "Educational Administration: Is It Unique?" School Review 67, no. 4 (Winter 1959): 461-68.

2. Roosevelt Johnson, "Black Administrators and Higher Education," Black Scholar 1 (November 1969): 66-76.

3. "Black Ph. D. s, " Transaction 7 (May 1970): 14.

4. Jacquelyne J. Jackson, "Black Ph. D.: Reply, " Transaction 7, no. 60 (October 1970): 6.

5. Harold M. Rose, "Appraisal of the Negro Educators' Situation in the Academic Market Place," Journal of Negro Education 35 (Winter 1966): 18-26.

6. Eddie W. Morris, "The Contemporary Negro College and the Brain Drain, " Journal of Negro Education 41 (Fall 1972): 309-19.

7. Earl E. Huyck, "Faculty in Predominantly White and Predominantly Negro Higher Institutions," Journal of Negro Education 25 (Fall 1966): 381-92.

8. David M. Rafky, "Attitudes of Black Scholars Toward Black Colleges," Journal of Negro Education 41 (Fall 1972): 320-30.

9. Wayman B. Shiver, Jr., "Black Professors: Salary or Service," Integrated Education 11 (July 1973): 56-57.

10. Kent G. Mommsen, "Black Ph. D. in the Academic Market Place: Supply and Demand and Price," Journal of Higher Education 45 (April 1974): 253-67.

11. Bennie L. Wiley, "A Different Breed of Administrator," Phi Delta Kappa 52 (April 1971): p. 55.

12. Bernard C. Watson, The Black Administrator in Higher Education: Current Dilemmas, Problems and Opportunities (Philadelphia: Temple University Press), April 1972.

13. Ibid.

14. "Cheek Brothers: A New Breed of College President," Ebony, October 1969, pp. 35-38.

15. Harvey R. HoHouser, "Comparative Attitudes Among College Administrators," Dissertation Abstracts International 32 (9-A) (March 1972): 4878.

16. Ibid., 4878.

17. Christopher Jencks and David Riesman, "American Negro Colleges: Future of the Negro Colleges," Harvard Educational Review 39 (Winter 1967): 43-60.

18. "New Black Presidents," Time, Decemver 27, 1968, pp. 48-49.

19. "Blacks in Higher Education: First Annual Report of the Institute for the Study of Educational Policy," Intellect 104 (April 1976): 486.

3

DESIGN AND PROCEDURES

This study was conducted during the 1977 calendar year to determine differences in the academic backgrounds and selected perceptions of black administrators working in predominantly black and predominantly white institutions of higher education in the United States and its territories and possessions.

CLASSIFICATION OF INSTITUTIONS OF HIGHER EDUCATION

In order to determine differences that might exist between black administrators working in black and white institutions of higher education, populations from land-grant institutions were used.*

---

*The basis for land-grant institutions dates back to the Northwest Ordinance of 1785. This ordinance made provision for granting tracts of federal land within the newer states for the support of "seminaries of higher learning." The Ordinance of 1787 permanently committed the United States to a system of public education. On July 2, 1862, Abraham Lincoln signed the Land-Grant Act, which was written and championed through Congress by Senator Justin S. Merrill of Vermont. The Land-Grant Act provided grants of federal land to every state that would agree to establish at least one college to teach agriculture, the mechanic arts, and scientific and classical subjects. The primary purpose for establishing colleges with such a broad curriculum was to provide a liberal and practical education and to make higher education accessible to all U.S. citizens (Facts 76, National Association of State Universities and Land-Grant Colleges, Suite 710, One Dupont Circle N.W., Washington, D.C. 20036).

These institutions were divided into two categories: black (60 percent or more of the student population) land-grant colleges and universities; and white land-grant colleges and universities. This division enabled the population of black administrators who work at black and white institutions of higher education to be determined. Tables 3.1 and 3.2 list the black and white land-grant institutions, respectively. Shown are the institution's name, location, and enrollment as of July 1, 1976.

Originally, this researcher had considered selecting the study population from all public institutions of higher education. That approach, however, was considered nonfeasible owing to the large number of institutions (approximately 3,000) and the time and cost limitations inherent. A second alternative for selecting institutions was to survey only large state-supported public institutions of higher education (5,000 or more students enrolled and working toward degrees). That approach was found to be unsatisfactory because of the relatively small size of most black institutions of higher education. Less than 10 state-supported black public higher institutions have a student population of 5,000 or more as compared to over 270 state-supported public white institutions in the same student population range. (See Tables C.1 and C.2 for listings of black and white institutions.)

A third alternative considered was to survey institutions that have adopted the "urban mission" as a philosophy of education in serving their constituents. However, this researcher could not find a singular definition of "urban mission" as expressed by various institutions around the nation. Moreover, the number of such institutions was found to be insufficient; institutions that express an "urban mission" philosophy are usually located in large urban and metropolitan areas, thus excluding most black institutions, which are traditionally located in small towns and rural areas of the southern, United States. (The only traditional black college located in the northern United States is Wilberforce University at Wilberforce, Ohio.)

Thus the decision was made to study land-grant institutions. All of the 50 states, as well as the District of Columbia, Guam, Puerto Rico, and the Virgin Islands, have at least one land-grant institution of higher education. Also, many states established white land-grant institutions and sister black land-grant institutions under the "separate but equal" doctrine of education that was established after the Civil War (see Table 3.3). There are 72 land-grant institutions of higher education, located in small towns of rural areas, medium-sized cities, and large metropolitan areas. Their student body populations range from approximately 1,000 to over 40,000.

TABLE 3.1

Black Land-Grant Institutions of Higher Education

Institution	Location	Enrollment
Alabama A&M University	Normal, Ala.	4,470
Alcorn State University	Lorman, Miss.	2,719
University of Arkansas at Pine Bluff	Pine Bluff, Ark.	2,556
Delaware State College	Dover, Del.	2,150
Florida A&M University	Tallahassee, Fla.	5,600
Fort Valley State College	Fort Valley, Ga.	1,862
Kentucky State University	Frankforth, Ky.	2,246
Langston University	Langston, Okla.	1,159
Lincoln University	Jefferson City, Mo.	2,485
University of Maryland (UMES)	Princess Anne, Md.	1,034
North Carolina A&M University	Greensboro, N.C.	5,209

(continued)

(Table 3.1   continued)

Institution	Location	Enrollment
Prairie View A&M University	Prairie View, Tex.	5,236
South Carolina State College	Orangeburg, S.C.	3,589
The Southern University System		
Southern University in Baton Rouge	Baton Rouge, La.	8,351
Southern University in New Orleans	New Orleans, La.	3,546
Southern University in Shreveport	Shreveport, La.	957
Tennessee State University	Nashville, Tenn.	5,128
Virginia State College	Petersburg, Va.	4,327
University of the District of Columbia	Washington, D.C.	7,774

Source: Office for Advancement of Public Negro Colleges, National Association of State Universities and Land-Grant Colleges, Atlanta, Georgia.

TABLE 3.2

White Land-Grant Institutions of Higher Education

Institution	Location	Enrollment
Auburn University	Auburn, Ala.	5,332
University of Alaska	Anchorage, Alaska	7,281
University of Arizona	Tucson, Ariz.	28,971
University of Arkansas	Fayetteville, Ark.	12,250
University of California System		
Berkeley	Berkeley, Calif.	28,278
Davis	Davis, Calif.	16,950
Irvine	Irvine, Calif.	8,622
Los Angeles	Los Angeles, Calif.	31,735
Riverside	Riverside, Calif.	5,129
San Diego	La Jolla, Calif.	9,428
Santa Barbara	Santa Barbara, Calif.	14,178
Santa Cruz	Santa Cruz, Calif.	6,105
Colorado State University	Fort Collins, Colo.	15,867
University of Connecticut	Storrs, Conn.	22,025
University of Delaware	Newark, Del.	12,600
University of Florida	Gainesville, Fla.	28,189
University of Georgia	Athens, Ga.	21,442
University of Guam	Agana, Guam	3,300
University of Hawaii	Honolulu, Hawaii	20,397

(continued)

(Table 3.2   continued)

Institution	Location	Enrollment
University of Idaho	Moscow, Idaho	8,134
University of Illinois	Urbana, Ill.	32,823
Purdue University	West Lafayette, Ind.	27,768
Iowa State University	Ames, Iowa	21,305
Kansas State University	Manhattan, Kan.	17,901
University of Kentucky	Lexington, Ky.	18,845
Louisiana State University	Baton Rouge, La.	22,693
University of Maine	Orono, Maine	10,513
University of Maryland	College Park, Md.	33,803
Massachusetts Institute of Technology	Cambridge, Mass.	8,482
University of Massachusetts	Amherst, Mass.	24,772
Michigan State University	East Lansing, Mich.	40,808
University of Minnesota	Minn.-St. Paul.	70,000

(Table 3.2   continued)

Institution	Location	Enrollment
Mississippi State University	Starkville, Miss.	11,709
University of Missouri	Columbia, Mo.	23,400
Montana State University	Bozeman, Mont.	8,002
University of Nebraska	Lincoln, Nebr.	20,892
University of Nevada	Reno, Nev.	8,225
University of New Hampshire	Durham, N.H.	9,800
Rutgers University	New Brunswick, N.J.	46,305
New Mexico State University	Las Cruces, N.Mex.	10,092
Cornell University	Ithaca, N.Y.	16,044
North Carolina State University	Raleigh, N.C.	16,542
North Dakota State University	Fargo, N. Dak.	6,957
Ohio State University	Columbus, Ohio	46,817
Oklahoma State University	Stillwater, Okla.	18,009

(Table 3.2   continued)

Institution	Location	Enrollment
Oregon State University	Corvallis, Oreg.	16,188
Pennsylvania State University	University Park, Pa.	70,767
University of Puerto Rico	Rio Piedras, Puerto Rico	25,719
University of Rhode Island	Kingston, R.I.	10,970
Clemson University	Clemson, S.C.	10,970
South Dakota State University	Brookings, S. Dak.	6,412
University of Tennessee	Knoxville, Tenn.	29,999
Texas A&M University	College Station, Tex.	24,293
Utah State University	Logan, Utah	8,926

(Table 3.2   continued)

Institution	Location	Enrollment
University of Vermont	Burlington, Vt.	8,287
College of the Virgin Islands	St. Thomas, Virgin Islands	1,893
Virginia Polytechnic Institute and State University	Blacksburg, Va.	18,477
Washington State University	Pullman, Wash.	15,637
West Virginia University	Morgantown, W. Va.	16,500
University of Wisconsin	Madison, Wis.	38,545
University of Wisconsin	Milwaukee, Wis.	23,596
University of Wyoming	Laramie, Wyo.	8,078

Source: Office for Advancement of Public Negro Colleges, National Association of State Universities and Land-Grant Colleges, Atlanta, Georgia.

TABLE 3.3

White Land-Grant Institutions and Sister
Black Land-Grant Institutions

State	Institution	Date of Establishment
Alabama	Auburn University	1856
	Alabama A&M University*	1875
Arkansas	University of Arkansas	1871
	University of Arkansas-Pine Bluff*	1873
Delaware	University of Delaware	1793
	Delaware State College*	1891
Florida	University of Florida	1853
	Florida A&M University*	1887
Georgia	University of Georgia	1785
	Fort Valley State College*	1895
Kentucky	University of Kentucky	1865
	Kentucky State University*	1886
Louisiana	Louisiana State University	1860
	Southern University*	1879
Maryland	University of Maryland	1807
	University of Maryland-Eastern Shore*	1886

(Table 3.3   continued)

State	Institution	Date of Establishment
Mississippi	Mississippi State University	1878
	Alcorn State University[*]	1871
Missouri	University of Missouri	1839
	Lincoln University[*]	1866
North Carolina	North Carolina State University	1887
	North Carolina A&M University[*]	1891
Oklahoma	Oklahoma State University	1890
	Langston University[*]	1897
South Carolina	Clemson University	1889
	South Carolina State College[*]	1895
Tennessee	University of Tennessee	1794
	Tennessee State University[*]	1909
Texas	Texas A&M University	1871
	Prairie View A&M University	1876
Virginia	Virginia Polytechnic Institute	1872
	Virginia State College[*]	1882

[*]Black institution.

Source: American Universities and Colleges: Eleventh Edition (Washington, D.C.: American Council on Education, 1973).

THE STUDY POPULATION

Using white land-grant colleges and universities and black land-grant colleges and universities as the criteria for the two-group classification, 189 black administrators in predominantly white institutions and 268 in predominantly black institutions were identified. The total research population was 457.

These study populations include all identified black administrators who hold the title of assistant dean or higher or equivalent title. As various institutions or groups of institutions use different title designations, this investigator asked, by telephone conversation and follow-up letters, that all institutions identify black administrators who hold titles appropriate to the parameters of this study. Tables 3.4 and 3.5 represent the frequencies and percentages in the various title categories for black administrators working at white and black land-grant institutions, respectively. At the level of president, chancellor, or provost, there are 18 black administrators at black institutions and 1 black administrator at white institutions, or 4.3 percent of the total study population. At the level of vice-president, vice-chancellor, or vice-provost, there are 36 black administrators at black institutions and 6 black administrators at white institutions for a total of 9.0 percent.

The smallest percentage of black administrators (2.1 percent) of the total population is at the level of assistant vice-president, assistant chancellor, or assistant provost.* At the level of registrar, manager, comptoller, or head librarian, there were 17 black administrators at black institutions and 3 black administrators at white institutions (4.3 percent). The highest percentage of black administrators was found at the level of dean, director, or divisional chairperson (43.0 percent), with 33 black administrators at white institutions and 165 black administrators at black institutions. Associate dean, associate director, associate division chairperson, and administrator level comprised 5.4 percent of the total population, including 21 black administrators at white institutions and 4 black administrators at black institutions. White institutions had 12 black administrators at the level of department chairperson, assistant to the president, assistant to the chancellor, or assistant to the provost. Black institutions had 18 black administrators at this level for a combined total of 7.0 percent of the total population. At the level of assistant dean,

---

*Many smaller colleges and universities do not use this title in their administrative hierarchy.

TABLE 3.4

Identification of Black Administrators at
White Land-Grant Institutions of Higher
Education by Frequency and Percentage

Title	Frequency	Percent
President, chancellor, provost	1	1.0
Vice-president, vice-chancellor, vice-provost	6	3.0
Assistant president, assistant chancellor, assistant provost	7	4.0
Registrar, manager, comptroller, head librarian, ombudsman	3	2.0
Dean, director, division chairperson	33	17.0
Associate dean, associate director, associate division chairperson, administrator	21	11.0
Department chairperson, assistant to the president, assistant to the chancellor, assistant to the provost	12	6.0
Assistant dean, coordinator, officer, assistant director	59	31.0

N = 189. Unidentified = 47 (25 percent).
Source: Compiled by the author.

TABLE 3.5

Identification of Black Administrators at
Black Land-Grant Institutions of Higher
Learning by Frequency and Percentage

Title	Frequency	Percent
President, chancellor, provost	18	6.7
Vice-president, vice-chancellor, vice-provost	36	13.4
Assistant vice-president, assistant chancellor, assistant provost	3	1.1
Registrar, manager, comptroller, head librarian	17	6.7
Dean, director, division chairperson	165	61.5
Associate dean, associate director, associate division chairperson, administrator	4	1.4
Department chairperson, assistant to the president, assistant to the chancellor, assistant to the provost	18	6.7
Assistant dean, coordinator, officer, assistant director	7	2.5

N = 268.
Source: Compiled by the author.

TABLE 3.6

Identification of Black Administrators at Black and White Land-Grant
Institutions of Higher Education by Frequencies and Percentages
in Eight Title Categories

Title	Frequency	Percent
President, chancellor, provost	19	4.3
Vice-president, vice-chancellor, vice-provost	42	9.0
Assistant vice-president, assistant chancellor, assistant vice-provost	10	2.1
Registrar, manager, comptroller, head librarian, ombudsman	20	4.4
Dean, director, division chairperson	198	43.0
Associate dean, associate director, associate division chairperson, administrator	25	5.4
Department chairperson, assistant to the president, assistant to the chancellor, assistant to the provost	30	7.0
Assistant dean, coordinator, officer, assistant director	66	14.4

N = 457. Unidentified = 47 (10.3 percent).
Source: Compiled by the author.

coordinator, officer, or assistant director, there were 59 black administrators at white institutions and 15 black administrators at black institutions (14.4 percent).

Out of a total population of 457 black administrators working at white and black land-grant institutions of higher education, 47, or 10.2 percent, could not be identified directly, as some institutions adhere to policies that do not allow individuals to be identified by criteria used for this study (these institutions only release information concerning faculty and staff that is consistent with the requirements of the Equal Employment Opportunity Commission's EEO-1 Form). However, those institutions did verify that the 47 respondents did fall within the title parameters used for this study. These respondents were forwarded the questionnaires through assigned officers at the respective institutions.

CRITERIA AND STUDY HYPOTHESES

After an extensive review of the literature relative to black administrators working at black and white institutions of higher education, this researcher found no criteria to ascertain differences in the career patterns of black administrators, and therefore constructed his own. The process followed entailed consulting with black experts in the field, which included black administrators and other black scholars around the nation. As a result, the following criteria were established: background characteristics, methods of recruitment and/or selection for administrative positions, professional characteristics, and opinions and perceptions toward employment.

Background Characteristics

Background information was obtained by asking black administrators to circle the appropriate items on the questionnaire relative to their age, sex, size of city of upbringing, their highest educational level, where they received their education, parents' educational and occupational levels, and their political and religious preferences.

Methods of Recruitment and/or Selection

Respondents were asked to circle the appropriate questionnaire item and to specify how they got their present administrative positions; what their reason was for leaving, if they were previously at a black institution; and from what source they learned about their present position. In addition, they were asked what importance they perceived race had in the decision to hire them; how much difficulty they had in getting their present position; and whether or not they were in a new position or filling a position vacancy.

Attitudes and Opinions Toward Present Employment

The respondents of this study were asked to answer a questionnaire item relative to the extent, in their opinion, to which racial discrimination existed in the hiring of black faculty and administrators at their respective institutions. They were also asked to respond to the amount of effort they perceived as being necessary to be promoted as compared to that of their white colleagues. Another question was how long they planned to remain at their present institution. The degree of professional satisfaction they derived from their present positions was also solicited. Further, they were asked whether or not they believed that their positions were created as a result of black student and/or affirmative action demands. Finally, they were asked to respond to the questionnaire item relating to their satisfaction with the amount of direct contact they have with black students.

Professional Characteristics

Professional characteristics covered items such as racial discrimination perceived relative to the respondents being hired and the effort perceived as being necessary to be promoted relative to that of white counterparts. The respondents were also asked to indicate how long they planned to remain at their present institution. They were also asked whether or not they were professionally satisfied with their present positions. Another question asked whether they believed that their jobs were created as a result of black students and/or affirmative action demands.

All these criteria were utilized to construct the hypotheses tested in this study (see Chapter 1).

QUESTIONNAIRE CONSTRUCTION

Following is a description of the steps taken to construct a questionnaire to gather data relevant to the hypotheses to be tested. First, scholars who have made nationwide studies relative to blacks in higher education were contacted. The questionnaires used by these scholars were requested for perusal by this researcher. After examining the questionnaires that were supplied by these scholars,[*] this investigator decided upon four content areas that would be necessary to gather data necessary to test the hypotheses: demographic and background data, methods of recruitment and/or selection by which black administrators obtained their present positions, professional characteristics, and attitudes and opinions toward present employment.

A preliminary questionnaire was prepared and distributed to a selected group of scholars for suggestions relative to the items and questions contained in the instrument.[†] A second draft of the instrument was then prepared and sent to the three scholars who had originally supplied the questionnaires used in their studies, for their comments and criticisms. The instrument was rewritten again with the incorporation of certain items, paraphrased, that had appeared in the questionnaires used in national studies by Kent G. Mommsen, William Moore, Jr., and Melvin Sykes.

Through the several revisions, the instrument length was shortened from 79 items to 67 items. It was finally determined that 52 items and questions were needed to procure information relative to the hypotheses of this study. That necessitated the construction of a six-page questionnaire. The questionnaire consisted of a letter of explanation of the rationale and intent of the study. This was followed by three pages with the 52 items printed on both sides of the pages. Also, the design tended to eliminate correlated material by having all criteria relevant to the questionnaire items arranged in logical and chronological sequence. Attention was given to the questionnaire format to ensure that the four categories of items correspond to the four hypotheses, respectively. Also, the conciseness of the questions and items should enable the respondents to complete the instrument with a minimum of time and effort. Questions and items

---

[*]Contributors of questionnaires for review were Kent G. Mommsen, Department of Sociology, University of Utah-Salt Lake City; William Moore, Jr., School of Education, Ohio State University; and Melvin Sykes, Department of Educational Psychology, University of Texas at Austin.

[†]Scholars who contributed suggestions for items and questions contained in the questionnaire were A. Chan, School of Education, University of Wisconsin-Milwaukee; Richard Larson, School of Education, University of Wisconsin-Milwaukee; Harold Rose, Department of Urban Affairs, University of Wisconsin-Milwaukee; and Ernest Spaights, Assistant Chancellor, University of Wisconsin-Milwaukee.

used in the questionnaire dealt directly with the purposes of this study.
The reader is referred to Appendix B for examination of the final
instrument.

ADMINISTRATION OF THE QUESTIONNAIRE

The questionnaire was administered to all black administrators
at land-grant institutions of higher education who hold the rank of
assistant dean or higher or equivalent ranks. To achieve this, initial contact was made with all land-grant institutions via telephone.
Institutions in Guam, Hawaii, Alaska, Puerto Rico, and the Virgin
Islands were contacted by mail initially. The purpose was to obtain
a listing of black administrators working at land-grant colleges and
universities. Therefore, the offices contacted at these institutions
were Institutional Research, Institutional Information Services, Affirmative Action, Public Relations, or Academic Affairs. The office
contacted at a given institution was usually suggested by the initial
contact at that institution, which was usually the Office of the President. All institutions were asked to supply information necessary to
contact black administrators to ask their cooperation for this study.
Once a mailing list was compiled and permissions were secured,
questionnaires were mailed to all the potential respondents. A letter
of explanation of purpose was mailed with all questionnaires (see Appendix A). A self-addressed, stamped envelope was also included.

A few (seven) land-grant institutions have policies that forbid
the dispensation of information relative to individual faculty members.
To facilitate the investigator in carrying out the study, these institutions were asked to designate a contact person through whom the
questionnaires could be distributed to the respondents. All institutions having such policies, except one, agreed to this procedure.

Each black administrator received a questionnaire with an
assigned code number stamped on its upper right-hand corner. This
was done to ensure anonymity to all persons other than the investigator, who, alone, could check identification by referring to a master
list of code numbers and associated names for purposes of follow-up
concerning questionnaire responses.

Code numbers were constructed so that the numbers of the
code represented the group, institution, and the administrator. The
farthest right three numerals represented the administrator. Moving
left, the next two numerals represented the institution. The left
numeral represented the group category. To ensure anonymity further, the two-numeral institutional identification appears on the master list but not on individual questionnaires. Thus, code number
1001 would mean the first contacted black administrator at a black

institution. If the corresponding number on the master list read 101001, this would mean that the respondent was the first respondent contacted at the first black institution on the list of black land-grant institutions. In this hypothetical case the respondent would have been the president of Alabama A&M University.

The questionnaire distribution began April 1, 1977 so that administrators would receive them at a time when spring recess was in progress at many institutions and also so that new administrators would have had as much time as possible on the job. Also, this investigator could still attempt to carry on the study within a planned time requirement. The follow-up mailings were done on June 1, 1977 and June 22, 1977.

INSTRUMENT VALIDITY AND RELIABILITY

Four hundred and fifty-seven black administrators were sent questionnaires; 320 responded, or 70 percent (see Table 3.7). Reasons for lack of response varied. For example, some administrators were on leave of absence and some black administrators had left their administrative positions and returned to teaching or had changed institutions and now worked at institutions that are not in the land-grant classification.

The returned questionnaires were checked for internal consistency of responses. For example, if an administrator checked "I have no teaching assignment" (Item 23, No. 4), this response was compared to the response to Item No. 29: "What percent of your

TABLE 3.7

Percentage of Questionnaire Returns by Black Administrators
Working at Black and White Land-Grant
Institutions of Higher Education

Black Institutions		White Institutions	Total
Number sent	268	189	457
Number returned	191	129	320
Percent returned	71.3	68.3	70

Source: Compiled by the author.

time is devoted to teaching?" Where discrepancies between such
responses occurred, the investigator telephoned the respondent to
get clarification. If the respondent could not be reached directly,
the institution was contacted in an effort to gain clarification of discrepancies between such responses. There were a total of eight
questionnaires that needed clarification to item responses therein.
Therefore, the internal consistency of the instrument was computed
at 96.1 percent.

Questionnaire responses were also checked against U.S. Census data relative to age category as a test of reliability. At a number
of institutions, questionnaires were sent to administrators who did
not have the title of assistant dean or higher or an equivalent rank.
The questionnaire responses were checked for internal consistency
as a further test of reliability. These responses were not included
in the study (N = 10).

METHODS EMPLOYED IN TESTING THE HYPOTHESES

The confidence level of significance used to evaluate differences in background characteristics and reject the null hypothesis
was $P = .05$. The tests used for each hypothesis follow.

1. No differences exist in the 14 variables of background characteristics of black administrators who work at black and white land-
   grant institutions of higher education.

This hypothesis was tested by arranging data into contingency tables
for the 14 variables that apply, the first 14 items of the questionnaire.
A chi-square test, with yates' correction for continuity where appropriate, was applied to each of the 14 variables to determine if there
were significant differences between black administrators working at
white land-grant institutions as compared to black administrators
working at black land-grant institutions. The data were analyzed by
statistical package for the social sciences (SPSS) computer pro-
gramming.*

2. No differences exist in the seven variables of the methods of recruitment and/or selection of black administrators who work at
   black and white land-grant institutions of higher education.

---

*The Statistical Package for the Social Sciences (SPSS) is a
computer language that will adequately handle nonparametric data.

Chi-square tests were used to compare the two groups on the seven variables of recruitment and/or selection of black administrators. The data were analyzed by SPSS.

3. No differences exist in the 24 variables of professional characteristics of black administrators who work at black and white land-grant institutions of higher education.

Chi-square tests were used to compare the two groups on the 24 variables of professional characteristics. SPSS was used to analyze the data.

4. No differences exist in the six variables of opinions and perceptions toward employment by black administrators who work at black and white land-grant institutions of higher education.

Chi-square tests were used to compare the two groups of black administrators on the six variables of attitudes and opinions toward present employment. SPSS was used to computer-analyze the data.

SUMMARY

Land-grant institutions of higher education were canvassed by telephone and mail in order to locate and identify black administrators who work in higher education. Through this procedure, 72 institutions were contacted and 457 black administrators were located. These administrators were classified into two groups: black administrators who work at black land-grant colleges and universities and black administrators who work at white land-grant colleges and universities.

Criteria for determining differences in the background and perceptions of the two groups of administrators were established. Variables were identified and applied to four areas pertinent to determining differences in background and perceptions of the administrators. Four hypotheses were then constructed that relate to the four criteria.

Questionnaires were constructed and mailed to all black administrators working at land-grant colleges and universities who hold the title of assistant dean or higher or equivalent title and to 10 administrators who were below the rank of assistant dean or equivalent in order to establish instrument reliability.

Responses from authorities in the field and the questionnaires that they submitted for perusal also aided in arriving at an instrument that is valid and reliable in the estimation of this researcher.

The hypotheses that were constructed relative to the background characteristics and selected perceptions of black administrators working at black and white land-grant institutions of higher education were tested by appropriate statistical procedures. Chapter 4 discusses the findings.

4

BACKGROUND CHARACTERISTICS

An hypothesis was constructed that stated that no differences exist in the 14 variables of background characteristics of black administrators who work at black and white land-grant institutions of higher education. The chi-square test was used to determine the validity of the hypothesis for each of the 14 variables at the 5 percent level of significance. The results were as follows.

AGE

If the history of black scholars on white campuses is recalled, only a miniscule number of black scholars had worked on white campuses prior to the mid-1960s. Once the brain drain started, as a result of the increased number of black students on white campuses, and the demands for programs that were relevant to the lives of black students, many white institutions were hard pressed to come up immediately with blacks to fill newly created positions. Therefore, many recent graduates from their own campuses were employed and oftentimes black individuals from nearby black communities were recruited. The older and more established black scholars were well aware of the impermanence that existed in many of the new positions and consequently were, in most cases, more difficult to recruit. One result of this is that at present black administrators at black institutions tend to be older than their counterparts at white institutions (see Table 4.1).

TABLE 4.1

Significance of Difference Between Black Administrators
Working at Black and White Land-Grant Institutions
of Higher Education Relating to Age

	Count	Type of Institution		Row Total
	Row Pc t	Black	White	
	Col Pc t			
Age	Total Pc t	1	2	
Less than 25	1.	0 .0 .0 .0	1 100.0 .8 .3	1 .3
25–29	2.	5 25.0 2.7 1.6	15 75.0 11.9 4.8	20 6.4
30–34	3.	18 51.4 9.7 5.8	17 48.6 13.5 5.4	35 11.2
35–39	4.	23 44.2 12.4 7.4	29 55.8 23.0 9.3	52 16.7
40–44	5.	26 53.1 14.0 8.3	23 46.9 18.3 7.4	49 15.7

(continued)

(Table 4.1   continued)

| Age | Count
Row Pc t
Col Pc t
Total Pc t | Type of Institution | | Row
Total |
| | | Black | White | |
		1	2	
45–49	6.	36 65.5 19.4 11.5	19 34.5 15.1 6.1	55 17.6
50–54	7.	33 70.2 17.7 10.6	14 29.8 11.1 4.5	47 15.1
55–59	8.	28 87.5 15.1 9.0	4 12.5 3.2 1.3	32 10.3
60–64	9.	12 75.0 6.5 3.8	4 25.0 3.2 1.3	16 5.1
65 and over	10.	5 100.0 2.7 1.6	0 .0 .0 .0	5 1.6
Column total		186 59.6	126 40.4	312 100.0

Chi square = 36.65715 with 9 degrees of freedom. Significance = .0000. Number of missing observations = 7.
Source: Compiled by the author.

SEX

There is no significant difference between black and white higher institutions relative to the ratio of black males to black females in administrative positions. At both black and white institutions, the numbers are slightly in favor of black males (see Table D.1).

SIZE OF CITY OF UPBRINGING

The size of the city lived in until and including 18 years of age reveals that black administrators at black institutions were raised in smaller cities than their counterparts at white institutions (see Table 4.2). This is not an arcane revelation, especially in light of the fact that until most recently black administrators were primarily to be found at the traditional black colleges and universities. The majority of these institutions were established in small cities in rural areas of the southern United States. Many black administrators have remained at their chosen black institutions for the majority of their professional careers. Conversely, and as previously stated, many black administrators at the white institutions have come from the same area where their employing institution is located. White institutions that have had the greatest proliferation of black students in the recent past and therefore have hired the majority of black administrators have been those institutions that are usually located in urban centers.

EDUCATIONAL LEVEL

There is no significant difference in the highest obtained educational level between black administrators at black institutions and black administrators at white institutions (see Table D.2). This might come as a surprise to many critics of black institutions as being inferior to white institutions. However, it should be clear that administering a black institution is no easier than administering a white institution. In fact, if resources are compared, the task of administering a black institution might be the more difficult.

UNDERGRADUATE DEGREE

The type of institution, black or white, where the black administrators received their undergraduate degrees was significantly different. Black administrators at black institutions predominantly

TABLE 4.2

Significance of Difference Between Black Administrators
Working at Black and White Land-Grant Institutions of
Higher Education Relating to Size of City Lived in
Before the Age of 18 Years

| | | Type of Institution | | |
Size City	Count Row Pc t Col Pc t Total Pc t	Black 1	White 2	Row Total
1. Under 25,000		99 73.9 52.9 31.8	35 26.1 28.1 11.3	134 43.1
2. 25,000– 40,000		20 66.7 10.7 6.4	10 33.3 8.1 3.2	30 9.6
3. 50,000– 99,000		15 44.1 8.0 4.8	19 55.9 15.3 6.1	34 10.9
4. 100,000– 499,000		30 50.0 16.0 9.6	30 50.0 24.2 9.6	60 19.3

(Table 4.2   continued)

	Count Row Pc t Col Pc t Total Pc t	Type of Institution		Row Total
Size City		Black 1	White 2	
500,000– 999,000	5.	12 50.0 6.4 3.9	12 50.0 9.7 3.9	24 7.7
1,000,000 and over	6.	11 37.9 5.9 3.5	18 62.1 14.5 5.8	29 9.3
Column total		187 60.1	124 39.9	311 100.0

Chi square = 24.29567 with 5 degrees of freedom. Significance = .0002. Number of missing observations = 8.

Source: Compiled by the author.

obtained their degrees from black institutions. The majority of black administrators at white institutions received their undergraduate degrees from white institutions (see Table 4.3). Again, consider the differences in age between the two groups of administrators. Also, remember the hostile environments on white campuses in the past.

MASTER'S DEGREE

When the two groups of black administrators were compared relating to what type of institution, black or white, at which they received their master's degrees, there was a significant difference. Sixty-nine and six-tenths percent of black administrators at black institutions received their master's degrees from white institutions as compared to 86.9 percent of their counterparts at white institutions (see Table 4.4). Again, this could not be considered unusual due to the fact that graduate education is not offered by many black institutions

Ph. D. DEGREE

A survey of black higher institutions will reveal that less than 10 offer Ph. D. s or other terminal degrees. Therefore, when the two groups of black administrators were compared relative to what type of institutions, black or white, at which they earned their Ph. D. s or other terminal degrees, there was no significant difference. Both groups predominantly received their terminal degrees from white institutions (see Table D.3).

PARENTS' HIGHEST EDUCATIONAL LEVEL

In comparing fathers' highest educational level and mothers' highest educational level between the two groups of black administrators, no attempt is being made to debate the controversy surrounding the effects of family background or heritability, the effects of which can be measured or estimated several different ways. The attempt made here was solely for the purpose of seeing if, in fact, the parents of one group might possibly have received more education than the parents of the other group. Taking into consideration that the administrators at black institutions appear to be older than their counterparts at white institutions might alone explain variances that might have been found in the level of the parents' education from one group to the other. However, there were no significant differences between the two groups of black administrators relative to fathers' highest

TABLE 4.3

Significance of Difference Between Black Administrators
Working at Black and White Land-Grant Institutions of
Higher Education Relating to the Type of Institution
Where They Earned Their Undergraduate Degrees

	Count	Type of Institution		Row Total
	Row Pc t	Black	White	
	Col Pc t			
Undergraduate Degree	Total Pc t	1	2	
Predominantly white	1.	16 19.0 8.5 5.1	68 81.0 54.8 21.8	84 26.9
Predominantly black	2.	172 75.4 91.5 55.1	56 24.6 45.2 17.9	228 73.1
Column total		188 60.3	124 39.7	312 100.0

Corrected chi-square = 79.17182 with 1 degree of freedom.
Significance = .0000. Number of missing observations = 7.
Source: Compiled by the author.

49

TABLE 4.4

Significance of Difference Between Black Administrators
Working at Black and White Land-Grant Institutions
of Higher Education Relating to Where
Earned Their Master's Degrees

Master's Degree	Count Row Pc t Col Pc t Total Pc t	Type of Institution		Row Total
		Black	White	
		1	2	
Predominantly white	1.	117 55.7 69.6 42.5	93 44.3 86.9 33.8	210 76.4
Predominantly black	2.	51 78.5 30.4 18.5	14 21.5 13.1 5.1	65 23.6
Column total		168 61.1	107 38.9	275 100.0

Corrected chi-square = 9.86935 with 1 degree of freedom.
Significance = .0017. Number of missing observations = 44.
Source: Compiled by the author.

educational level or mothers' highest educational level (see Tables
D.4 and D.5).

FATHERS' OCCUPATIONAL LEVEL

For this variable, a comparison of the two groups of black administrators resulted in a chi-square of 4.464 and a significance of
.4846. This indicated that the null hypothesis was supported and that
there was no significant difference in fathers' occupational levels.
These data are summarized in Table D.6.

MOTHERS' OCCUPATIONAL LEVEL

In comparing the two groups of black administrators relative
to this variable, a chi-square of 9.170 and a significance of .1025
resulted, indicating that no significant difference existed between the
two groups (see Table D.7).

POLITICAL PREFERENCE

When the two groups of black administrators were compared
relative to their political preferences, a chi-square of 15.96 and a
significance of .0012 resulted, indicating a significant difference between the two groups. For black administrators at black land-grant
institutions, 84.9 percent were Democrats, 0.5 percent were Repub-
licans, 13 percent were Independents, and 1.6 percent had other
political preferences. For black administrators at white land-grant
institutions, 65.9 percent were Democrats, 2.4 percent were Repub-
licans, 29.4 percent were Independents, and 2.4 percent held other
political preferences. A summary of political preferences can be
found in Table 4.5.

POLITICAL VIEWS

For the variable political views, the null hypothesis was not
supported. A comparison of the two groups of black administrators
resulted in a chi-square of 16.63 and a significance of .0053, indicating that there was a significant difference between the two groups.
For black administrators at black institutions, 2.7 percent
viewed themselves as "extreme left," 34.6 percent were "left of center" (liberal), 57.7 percent were "moderate," 3.3 percent were "right

TABLE 4.5

Significance of Difference Between Black Administrators
Working at Black and White Land-Grant Institutions of
Higher Education Relating to Their Political Preference

		Type of Institution		
	Count			
	Row Pc t	Black	White	Row Total
Political	Col Pc t			
Preference	Total Pc t	1	2	
Democrat	1.	157 65.4 84.9 50.5	83 34.6 65.9 26.7	240 77.2
Republican	2.	1 25.0 .5 .3	3 75.0 2.4 1.0	4 1.3
Independent	3.	24 39.3 13.0 7.7	37 60.7 29.4 11.9	61 19.6
Other	4.	3 50.0 1.6 1.0	3 50.0 2.4 1.0	6 1.9
Column total		185 59.5	126 40.5	311 100.0

Chi-square = 15.96896 with 3 degrees of freedom. Significance = .0012. Number of missing observations = 8.

Source: Compiled by the author.

of center" (conservative), 0.5 percent were "extreme right," and 1.1 percent were "other." For black administrators at white institutions, 2.5 percent viewed themselves as "extreme left," 54.1 percent were "left of center" (liberal), 36.1 percent were "moderate," 2.5 percent were "right of center" (conservative), 0.8 percent were "extreme right," and 4.1 percent were "other" (see Table 4.6).

RELIGIOUS PREFERENCE

Comparing the two groups of black administrators for religious preference resulted in a chi-square of 13.20 and a significance of .0042, indicating that the null hypothesis should be rejected. The findings for black administrators at black institutions showed: Protestant, 53.7 percent; Roman Catholic, 3.8 percent; Black Muslim, 0.5 percent; and other religious preferences, 3.9 percent. The findings for black administrators at white institutions: Protestants, 29.6 percent; Roman Catholic, 7.4 percent; Black Muslim, 0.0 percent; and other religious preferences, 18.0 percent. See Table 4.7 for a complete description.

In summary, the hypothesis that no differences exist in the 14 variables of background characteristics of black administrators who work at black and white institutions of higher education was supported for seven variables: sex, educational level, where they received their Ph.D.s or other terminal degrees, fathers' highest educational levels, mothers' highest educational levels, fathers' occupational levels, and mothers' occupational levels. The hypothesis was rejected for the seven variables: age, size of city of upbringing, where they received their undergraduate degrees, where they received their master's degrees, political preferences, their political views, and their religious preferences.

TABLE 4.6

Significance of Difference Between Black Administrators
Working at Black and White Land-Grant Institutions of
Higher Education Relating to Their Political Views

| | Count | Type of Institution | | Row Total |
Political Views	Row Pc t Col Pc t Total Pc t	Black 1	White 2	
1. Extreme left		5 62.5 2.7 1.6	3 37.5 2.5 1.0	8 2.6
2. Left of center		63 48.8 34.6 20.7	66 51.2 54.1 21.7	129 42.4
3. Moderate		105 70.5 57.7 34.5	44 29.5 36.1 14.5	149 3.0
4. Right of center		6 66.7 3.3 2.0	3 33.3 2.5 1.0	9 3.0

(Table 4.6   continued)

| | | Type of Institution | | |
Political Views	Count Row Pc t Col Pc t Total Pc t	Black 1	White 2	Row Total
Extreme right	5.	1 50.0 .5 .3	1 50.0 .8 .3	2 .7
Other	6.	2 28.6 1.1 .7	5 71.4 4.1 1.6	7 2.3
Column total		182 59.9	122 40.1	304 100.0

Chi square = 16.63452 with 5 degrees of freedom. Significance = .0053. Number of missing observations = 15.

Source: Compiled by the author.

TABLE 4.7

Significance of Difference Between Black Administrators
Working at Black and White Land-Grant Institutions of
Higher Education Relating to Their Religious Preference

Religious Preference	Count Row Pc t Col Pc t Total Pc t	Type of Institution		Row Total
		Black 1	White 2	
Protestant	1.	165 64.5 89.2 53.7	91 35.5 74.6 29.6	240 83.4
Roman Catholic	2.	7 43.8 3.8 2.3	9 56.3 7.4 2.9	16 5.2
Black Muslim	4.	1 100.0 .5 .3	0 .0 .0 .0	1 .3
Other	5.	12 35.3 6.5 3.9	22 64.7 18.0 7.2	34 11.1
Column total		185 60.3	122 39.7	307 100.0

Chi-square = 13.20975 with 3 degrees of freedom. Significance =
.0042. Number of missing observations = 12.

Source: Compiled by the author.

5

METHODS OF RECRUITMENT
AND/OR SELECTION

A second hypothesis was constructed that stated no difference exists in the seven variables of the methods of recruitment and/or selection of black administrators who work at black and white land-grant institutions of higher education. The chi-square test was used to determine the validity of the hypothesis for each of the seven variables at the 5 percent level of significance. The following describes the results.

HOW THEY GOT THEIR POSITIONS

The methods through which black administrators got their positions were significantly different at black land-grant institutions as compared to white land-grant institutions. At black institutions many of the black administrators came up through the ranks to their present positions. Many of them remained at the same institutions for many years as a result of the satisfaction with their overall working conditions, even though in many instances as they ascended through the ranks they were required to wear many hats. That is, they were often required to teach, fund raise, and carry out administrative duties.

Some of the black administrators were recruited from other black institutions. However, considering that in retrospect the black institutions were primarily where the black academicians were to be found and that they still remain the focal point of black education, the black institutions were logically the place to recruit black scholars. The brain drain would also give credence to that assumption. The collegial interactions and mutual concerns within the field would also provide the opportunity for the administrations and faculties of black institutions to become well acquainted with each other. It is known that in times past athletic competition of black institutions came from other black institutions. It is also known that there was little exchange between the black and white academic communities.

At white land-grant institutions, many of the black administrators got their present positions by applying for vacancies. This is not to say that recruitment of black scholars to white campuses ceased when the white institutions were accused of draining prime talent from the black institutions. It does say, however, that once white institutions filled their predetermined quotas of blacks, they ceased to look further and were more inclined to say that black scholars and administrators could not be located rather than to provide opportunities for training and development. (See Table 5.1.)

REASONS FOR LEAVING

If previously employed at a black institution, the respondents were asked to list their reasons for leaving. At black land-grant institutions, many of the black administrators were recruited from other black institutions. Some changed black institutions for advancement on their own initiative. Commonly educators often have a desire to relocate in different geographical areas. And often more suitable working conditions can be found by changing institutions.

At white land-grant institutions, fewer black administrators were recruited from black institutions as compared to black land-grant institutions. Many black administrators changed from other white institutions for reasons related to advancement. Most recently, many black administrators change from one white institution to another because of the tenuous nature of their positions. It is also noted that 21.1 percent of black administrators at black institutions and 59.8 percent of black administrators at white institutions did not come from black institutions.

At the time this survey was conducted, there was only one black administrator at a white land-grant institution who held the rank of president, chancellor, or provost. At the level of vice-president, vice-chancellor, or vice-provost, there were only six blacks at white land-grant institutions. Therefore, it is safe to assume that blacks who are leaving black institutions and going to white institutions, regardless of the reasons, are not walking into top administrative positions. Those blacks who are gaining top posts at white institutions could just as well run AT&T, Standard Oil, or General Motors, if given the chance. (See Table 5.2.)

TABLE 5.1

Significance of Difference Between Black Administrators
Working at Black and White Land-Grant Institutions of
Higher Education Relating to How They Got Their Positions

| Got Position | Count Row Pc t Col Pc t Total Pc t | Type of Institution | | Row Total |
		Black 1	White 2	
1. Was recruited		99 60.7 52.7 31.5	64 39.3 50.8 20.4	163 51.9
2. Applied for vacancy		42 47.2 22.3 13.4	47 52.8 37.3 15.0	89 28.3
3. General application		10 71.4 5.3 3.2	4 28.6 3.2 1.3	14 4.5
4. Other		37 77.1 19.7 11.8	11 22.9 8.7 3.5	48 15.3
Column total		188 59.9	126 40.1	314 100.0

Chi-square = 12.70427 with 3 degrees of freedom. Significance =
.0053. Number of missing observations = 5.

Source: Compiled by the author.

TABLE 5.2

Significance of Difference Between Black Administrators
Working at Black and White Land-Grant Institutions
of Higher Education Relating to Reasons
for Leaving Black Institutions

Leaving Black Institution	Count Row Pc t Col Pc t Total Pc t	Type of Institution		Row Total
		Black	White	
		1	2	
Was recruited	1.	39 75.0 30.5 18.6	13 25.0 15.9 6.2	52 24.8
Sought position	2.	14 87.5 10.9 6.7	2 12.5 2.4 1.0	16 7.6
Not from black institution	3.	27 35.5 21.1 12.9	49 64.5 59.8 23.3	76 36.2
Other	4.	48 72.7 37.5 22.9	18 27.3 22.0 8.6	66 31.4
Column total		128 61.0	82 39.0	210 100.0

Chi-square = 33.53780 with 3 degrees of freedom. Significance = .0000. Number of missing observations = 109.
<u>Source:</u> Compiled by the author.

LEARNED OF POSITION

This variable relates to the source from which the respondents learned about their present positions. When the two groups of black administrators were compared, a chi-square of 23.60 and a significance of 0.0013 resulted, thus indicating that a significant difference existed between the two groups.

At black land-grant institutions, many of the black administrators learned about their present positions from friends or professional colleagues. Also, many black administrators were sought by the heads of the black institutions. At white land-grant institutions, although to a lesser degree than at black land-grant institutions, many of the black administrators learned about their present positions from friends or professional colleagues. Black administrators at white land-grant institutions in some instances were found through search and screen committees. Table 5.3 gives a full description of the findings for this variable.

RACE VERSUS PROFESSIONAL QUALIFICATIONS

This variable relates to the perceptions of what importance race, as compared to professional qualifications, played in the hiring of black administrators. A comparison of the two groups of black administrators resulted in a chi-square of 34.53 and a significance of 0.000, indicating that there was a significant difference between the two groups. Race or race in combination with professional qualifications seems to have been more important at white land-grant institutions. When hiring a black administrator, white institutions usually look for impeccable credentials and an extensive track record. Also, in some respects, the individual must be considered "safe." (See Table 5.4.)

DIFFICULTY

Relative to the amount of difficulty black administrators had in getting their present positions, a chi-square of 8.65 and a significance of 0.0132 indicated that the two groups of black administrators differed in the difficulty experienced in getting their present positions. Black administrators at white institutions had more difficulty in getting their present positions. In some instances, it has been revealed that administrators who sought positions at white institutions experienced negative results one or more times before they were hired.

TABLE 5.3

Significance of Difference Between Black Administrators
Working at Black and White Land–Grant Institutions
of Higher Education Relating to How They Learned
About Their Present Position

Learned of Position	Count Row Pc t Col Pc t Total Pc t	Type of Institution		Row Total
		Black	White	
		1	2	
1. Graduate degree	1.	5 55.6 2.9 1.7	4 44.4 3.2 1.3	9 3.0
2. Graduate school	2.	1 50.0 .6 .3	1 50.0 .8 .3	2 .7
3. Friend or colleague	3.	98 66.7 57.0 33.0	49 33.3 39.2 16.5	147 49.5
4. Newspaper ads	4.	1 11.1 .6 .3	1 88.9 6.4 2.7	9 3.0
5. University placement	5.	1 14.3 .6 .3	6 85.7 4.8 2.0	7 2.5

(Table 5.3   continued)

		Type of Institution		
	Count			Row Total
	Row Pc t	Black	White	
Learned of Position	Col Pc t			
	Total Pc t	1	2	
Private agency	6.	0 .0 .0 .0	1 100.0 .8 .3	1 2.4
Mass letter or announcement	7.	4 30.8 2.3 1.3	9 69.2 7.2 3.0	13 4.4
Other	8.	62 56.9 36.0 20.9	47 43.1 37.6 15.8	109 36.7
Column total		172 15.9	125 42.1	297 100.0

Chi-square = 23.60094 with 7 degrees of freedom. Significance = .0013. Number of missing observations = 22.

Source: Compiled by the author.

TABLE 5.4

Significance of Difference Between Black Administrators
Working at Black and White Land-Grant Institutions
of Higher Education Relating to the Perceived
Importance of Race Versus Professional
Qualifications in Their Being Hired

Race Versus Professional Qualification	Count Row Pc t Col Pc t Total Pc t	Type of Institution		Row Total
		Black 1	White 2	
90–10	1.	24 68.6 16.8 9.2	11 31.4 9.3 4.2	35 13.4
70–30	2.	4 20.0 2.8 1.5	16 80.0 13.6 6.1	20 7.7
50–50	3.	34 43.0 23.8 13.0	45 57.0 38.1 17.2	79 30.3
30–70	4.	12 36.4 8.4 4.6	21 63.6 17.8 8.0	33 12.6
10–90	5.	69 73.4 48.3 26.4	25 26.6 21.2 9.6	94 36.0
Column total		143 54.8	118 45.2	261 100.0

Chi-square = 34.53270 with 4 degrees of freedom. Significance =
.0000. Number of missing observations = 58.
Source: Compiled by the author.

Being told that one is one of the final two or three persons considered for a position does nothing for one's personal economics.

Black administrators at black institutions had less difficulty in securing positions, even though black institutions number only approximately 120 versus thousands of white higher institutions. (See Table 5.5.)

REASONS FOR DIFFICULTY

The perceived reasons for the difficulty in getting present positions range from the present leveling off in student enrollment to black administrators being told that they were not considered because of the institution's assessment that the surrounding environment would be unconducive to their professional growth and development. Many institutions that advertise as equal opportunity employers have no black or other minorities on their faculties or in their administrations. However, there was no significant difference between the two groups of black administrators in their perceptions as to the reasons for the difficulty in getting their positions. It is also noted that only 79 out of 319 administrators responded to this questionnaire item (see Table E.1).

NEW OR VACANT POSITION

This variable relates to the type of position being filled by black administrators. When the two groups of administrators were compared, a chi-square of 4.21 and a significance of .1216 resulted. Therefore, the null hypothesis was supported. Table E.2 gives a description of the findings for this variable.

In summary, the hypothesis that no differences exist in the seven variables of the methods of recruitment and/or selection of black administrators who work at black and white institutions of higher education was supported for two variables: perceived reasons for difficulty in obtaining present positions and the type of positions being filled—new positions or position vacancies. The hypothesis was rejected for five variables: how administrators got their present positions; reason for leaving, if previously employed at a black institution; how black administrators learned about their present positions; race versus professional qualifications; and difficulty in getting their positions.

TABLE 5.5

Significance of Difference Between Black Administrators
Working at Black and White Land-Grant Institutions
of Higher Education Relating to the Difficulty in
Getting Their Present Position

	Count Row Pc t Col Pc t Total Pc t	Type of Institution		Row Total
Difficulty		Black 1	White 2	
Great	1.	2 100.0 1.2 .7	0 .0 .0 .0	2 .7
Some	2.	13 37.1 7.5 4.4	22 62.9 17.9 7.4	35 11.8
Little	3.	158 61.0 91.3 53.4	101 39.0 ·82.1 34.1	259 87.5
Column total		173 58.4	123 41.6	296 100.0

Chi-square = 8.65984 with 2 degrees of freedom. Significance=
.0132. Number of missing observations = 23.
Source: Compiled by the author.

6

DIFFERENCES IN PROFESSIONAL CHARACTERISTICS

The third hypothesis constructed stated that no differences exist in 24 variables of professional characteristics of black administrators who work at black and white institutions of higher education. The chi-square test was used to determine the validity of the hypothesis for each of 24 variables at the five percent level of significance. A description of the results follows.

ACADEMIC RANK

Whether or not there would be differences in academic rank between black administrators at black and white institutions might have been considered obvious. However, in the interest of satisfying inquiry into the effects of the recently employed black academicians on white campuses, this variable was explored. In many spheres, black institutions had long been considered the residuals of "separate but equal" education. Very little concern was given to black institutions with the exception that they provided an avenue to keep the majority of black students off white campuses until the mid-1960s. It is doubtful whether full realization was given to the vital role these black institutions played in providing education for the largest ethnic group in the United States. As a result, black academicians usually served their full careers at black institutions.

Presently, black administrators are two years older than the national average of all administrators, coupled with the fact that very few new black administrators are being hired by white institutions. Also, with integration, black institutions are not increasing appreciably the numbers of black administrators being hired. The integration of the faculties and staffs of black institutions is a noble ideal.

However, the same zeal is not evidenced in the integration of the faculties and staffs of white higher educational institutions. Consequently, black administrators at black institutions have acquired higher rank than black administrators at white institutions. (See Table 6.1.)

STABILITY OF POSITION

Not only is getting administrative positions in higher education difficult for blacks but having the opportunity to build a secure and stable future is also a matter of grave concern for most black administrators at white institutions as compared to black administrators at black institutions. Many recently arrived black administrators on white campuses were hired into impermanent positions, this condition in most instances being known when the position was secured. However, there should be opportunity to increase one's future prospects in capacities other than answering complaints against the institution in the minority affairs area or addressing black student grievances. Most assuredly, those black individuals who are hired at the dean level or above often bargain for tenure as one of the conditions of their employment. Other black individuals who are employed in lesser positions are not in a position to bargain for tenure at the outset of their employment. When the administrative appointment conditions change, these individuals in most instances have not accrued departmental seniority and often, after having spent five, six, or seven years at a given institution, must begin the appointment quest anew.

Tenure is less likely for black administrators at white institutions than for their counterparts at black institutions. Also, with the advent of most black administrators at white institutions having positions that are entirely administrative, they are less likely to gain tenure. Perhaps having to "wear many hats" has some advantage after all. For a more detailed statistical account, see Table 6.2.

TYPES OF STUDENTS TAUGHT

There were no significant differences in the types of students taught by the two groups of administrators. That is, whether or not the administrators taught undergraduates, graduates, or a combination of both was not significantly different. However, from the foregoing, it is known that black administrators at black institutions do considerably more teaching than their counterparts at white institutions. From that and the fact that white institutions offer more

TABLE 6.1

Significance of Difference Between Black Administrators
Working at Black and White Land-Grant Institutions of
Higher Education Relating to Their Academic Rank

Academic Rank	Count Row Pc t Col Pc t Total Pc t	Type of Institution		Row Total
		Black 1	White 2	
Professor	1.	76 82.6 40.9 24.4	16 17.4 12.7 5.1	92 29.5
Associate professor	2.	24 60.0 12.9 7.7	16 40.0 12.7 5.1	40 12.8
Assistant professor	3.	17 54.8 9.1 5.4	14 45.2 11.1 4.5	31 9.3

(continued)

(Table 6.1   continued)

Academic Rank	Count Row Pc t Col Pc t Total Pc t	Type of Institution		Row Total
		Black	White	
		1	2	
Instructor	4.	2 66.7 1.1 .6	1 33.3 .8 .3	3 1.0
Administrator only	5.	62 47.3 33.3 19.9	69 52.7 54.8 22.1	131 42.0
Other	6.	5 33.3 2.7 1.6	10 66.7 7.9 3.2	15 4.8
Column total		186 59.6	126 40.4	312 100.0

Chi-square = 33.07970 with 5 degrees of freedom. Significance = .0000. Number of missing observations = 7.

Source: Compiled by the author.

TABLE 6.2

Significance of Difference Between Black Administrators
Working at Black and White Land–Grant Institutions
of Higher Education Relating to the
Stability of Their Positions

		Type of Institution		
		---	---	
	Count			Row Total
	Row Pc t	Black	White	
Stability of Position	Col Pc t			
	Total Pc t	1	2	
Tenured	1.	92	35	127
		72.4	27.6	42.1
		50.3	29.4	
		30.5	11.6	
Tenure-tracked	2.	17	8	25
		68.0	32.0	8.3
		9.3	6.7	
		5.6	2.6	
Not tenure-tracked	3.	73	76	149
		49.0	51.0	49.3
		39.9	63.9	
		24.2	25.2	
Other	4.	1	0	1
		100.0	.0	.3
		.5	.0	
		.3	.0	
Column total		183	119	302
		60.6	39.4	100.0

Chi-square = 17.08757 with 3 degrees of freedom. Significance =
.0007. Number of missing observations = 17.
Source: Compiled by the author.

course work at the graduate level than their counterpart black institutions, one might well have assumed that there would be a difference in the types of students taught (see Table F.1).

LENGTH OF YEARLY APPOINTMENT

When the two groups of administrators were compared, the null hypothesis was supported. A chi-square of 4.40 and a significance of 0.1107 indicated that there was no significant difference in the length of yearly appointments held by the two groups of black administrators. Administrative appointments for these administrators were overwhelmingly the standard 12-month or annual appointments that are usual for college administration. With these appointments come the 20 working days of vacation. Administrators are quick to point out that individuals who are allowed to take 20 consecutive days of vacation are truly fortunate. That withstands, regardless of the type of institution, black or white, or the color of the administrator. Table F.2 gives a complete description.

ANNUAL SALARY

Table F.3 shows that the null hypothesis was supported when the two groups of administrators were compared relative to salary. It comes as a surprise that there are no significant differences in the salaries paid to black administrators at both black and white land-grant institutions. The high salaries that were offered to attract black scholars to white campuses during the brain drain era seem not to have had an effect on the overall salary averages of the two groups of administrators. However, if teaching faculties at the two types of institutions were compared relative to salaries, there would undoubtedly be differences.

TIME IN POSITION

The length of time that the two groups of administrators have been in their present positions was significantly different, as expected. Black administrators at black institutions had more seniority in their positions than their counterparts at white institutions. At the present low rate at which blacks are being tenure at white institutions nationally, the gap between the number of tenured administrators at black and white institutions will undoubtedly widen in the future.

At white institutions, 57.3 percent of black administrators have three years or less seniority in their positions. Slightly over 25 percent of black administrators at white land-grant institutions have between four and six years seniority in their positions. Of all black administrators at white land-grant institutions, 97.6 percent have less than ten years in their present positions. In comparison, 83.3 percent of black administrators at black institutions have been in their present positions for less than ten years. (See Table 6.3.)

RESEARCH AND WRITING

The percentage of time devoted to research and writing was not significantly different between the two groups of administrators. As expected, administrators in the two groups do less research and writing than teaching faculty. However, in many instances, the administrators at both types of institutions have remained productive of research and writing. The uniqueness and the demands of higher education administration do not afford much time to do other than position-related activities. Table F.4 gives a complete description of this variable.

TEACHING

There was a significant difference in the amount of time devoted to teaching. When the two groups of administrators were compared, black administrators at black institutions spent more time teaching than their counterparts at white institutions. At black institutions, administrators often are required to teach a class. And many of them teach as a matter of choice as a result of being in positions whereby they are exposed to the economic realities of their institutions. (See Table 6.4.)

ADMINISTRATION

The percentage of time devoted to administration did not differ significantly between the two groups of administrators. However, as previously stated, the additional duties that have to be performed by administrators are much greater at black institutions. When the two groups of administrators were compared, a chi-square of 11.20 and a significance of 0.2624 resulted (see Table F.5).

TABLE 6.3

Significance of Difference Between Black Administrators
Working at Black and White Land-Grant Institutions
of Higher Education Relating to the Length of Time
They Have Been in Their Present Positions

		Type of Institution		
Time in Position (Years)	Count Row Pc t Col Pc t Total Pc t	Black 1	White 2	Row Total
0-3	1.	87 55.1 46.8 28.1	71 44.9 57.3 22.9	158 51.0
4-6	2.	30 48.4 16.1 9.7	32 51.6 25.8 10.3	62 20.0
7-9	3.	38 67.9 20.4 12.3	18 32.1 14.5 5.8	56 18.1
10-12	4.	11 91.7 5.9 3.5	1 8.3 .8 .3	12 3.9

(Table 6.3   continued)

| Time in Position (Years) | Count Row Pc t Col Pc t Total Pc t | Type of Institution | | Row Total |
		Black 1	White 2	
13-15	5.	9 100.0 4.8 2.9	0 .0 .0 .0	9 2.9
Over 15	6.	11 84.6 5.9 3.5	2 15.4 1.6 .6	13 4.2
Column total		186 60.0	124 40.0	310 100.0

Chi-square = 20.82472 with 5 degrees of freedom. Significance = .0009. Number of missing observations = 9.

Source: Compiled by the author.

TABLE 6.4

Significance of Difference Between Black Administrators
Working at Black and White Land-Grant Institutions
of Higher Education Relating to the Percentage of
Time Devoted to Teaching

| Teaching Time (percent) | Count Row Pc t Col Pc t Total Pc t | Type of Institution | | Row Total |
		Black 1	White 2	
0-9	1.	115 58.1 65.3 38.7	83 41.9 68.6 27.9	198 66.7
10-19	2.	20 46.5 11.4 6.7	23 53.5 19.0 7.7	43 14.5
20-29	3.	14 56.0 8.0 4.7	11 44.0 9.1 3.7	25 8.4
30-39	4.	9 81.8 5.1 3.0	2 18.2 1.7 .7	11 3.7
40-49	5.	7 100.0 4.0 2.4	0 .0 .0 .0	7 2.4
50-59	6.	5 83.3 2.8 1.7	1 16.7 .8 .3	6 2.0

(Table 6.4   continued)

	Count	Type of Institution		Row Total
	Row Pc t	Black	White	
Teaching Time (percent)	Col Pc t			
	Total Pc t	1	2	
60–69	7.	4	0	4
		100.0	.0	1.3
		2.3	.0	
		1.3	.0	
70–79	8.	1	0	1
		100.0	.0	.3
		.6	.0	
		.3	.0	
80–89	9.	0	1	1
		.0	100.0	.3
		.0	.8	
		.0	.3	
90–100	10.	1	0	1
		100.0	.0	.3
		.6	.0	
		.3	.0	
Column total		176	121	297
		59.3	40.7	100.0

Chi-square = 17.26927 with 9 degrees of freedom. Significance = .0447. Number of missing observations = 22.

Source: Compiled by the author.

COMMUNITY SERVICE

The percentage of time devoted to community service differed significantly between the two groups of administrators. Black administrators at white institutions devote more time to community service than their counterparts at black institutions. How much the level of community service is influenced by the three-part mission of teaching, research/writing, and community service is taken into consideration when granting tenure or promotion at most white institutions is not known. However, many black administrators at white institutions express that some of their community service is directed toward making more frequent contact with black communities.

There has also been accusation that black institutions do not provide enough extension service to their immediate surrounding communities. Also, they are said not to provide enough research with a regional focus. (See Table 6.5.)

FUNDING FOR POSITIONS

The sources from which the administrators' positions derived their funding, that is, outside funding (soft money) and institutional funds (hard money), were not significantly different. At both types of institutions, less than 10 percent of the black administrators relied on securing outside funds for their positions. However, this is not to say that soft money does not create some positions at both types of institutions. At black institutions in many instances the procurement of Advanced Institutional Development Program (AIDP) funds have made possible the employment of administrators in critical areas. Usually AIDP funds are granted over a five-year period that is designed to accelerate institutional development. More recently, both types of institutions have availed themselves of AIDP funds. Obviously, there are other sources of soft money—too many to enumerate here (see Table F.6).

JOBS DEPENDENT UPON

Whether or not the positions held by the two groups of administrators were dependent upon their own ability or the institutions' ability to raise outside funds might at first seem repetitious of the foregoing statement relative to the sources from which the two groups of administrative positions derived their funding. However, this is not the case. In some instances, individuals, through their ability to develop and write proposals, have been able to create positions that

TABLE 6.5

Significance of Difference Between Black Administrators
Working at Black and White Land-Grant Institutions
of Higher Education Relating to the Percentage of
Time Devoted to Community Service

		Type of Institution		
	Count			
		Black	White	Row Total
	Row Pc t			
Community Service Time (percent)	Col Pc t			
	Total Pc t	1	2	
0-9	1.	86 68.8 58.9 29.0	39 31.2 32.2 13.1	125 42.1
10-19	2.	59 56.2 33.5 19.9	46 43.8 38.0 15.5	105 35.4
20-29	3.	13 43.3 7.4 4.4	17 56.7 14.0 5.7	30 10.1
30-39	4.	8 53.3 4.5 2.7	7 46.7 5.8 2.4	15 5.1
40-49	5.	3 50.0 1.7 1.0	3 50.0 2.5 1.0	6 2.0

(continued)

(Table 6.5   continued)

Community Service Time (percent)	Count Row Pc t Col Pc t Total Pc t	Type of Institution		Row Total
		Black	White	
		1	2	
50–59	6.	5 71.4 2.8 1.7	2 28.6 1.7 .7	7 2.4
60–69	7.	0 .0 .0 .0	1 100.0 .8 .3	1 .3
70–79	8.	0 .0 .0 .0	1 100.0 .8 .3	1 .3
80–89	9.	1 100.0 .6 .3	0 .0 .0 .0	1 .3
90–100	10.	1 16.7 .6 .3	5 83.3 4.1 1.7	6 2.0
Column total		176 59.3	121 40.7	297 100.0

Chi-square = 17.23994 with 9 degrees of freedom. Significance = .0451. Number of missing observations = 22.
Source: Compiled by the author.

would not otherwise exist. Often, positions of this type depend upon the continuing ability to develop proposals and secure funds. At the institutional level some positions are created as a result of institutional grants from the National Science Foundation or Ford Foundation, for example. However, a comparison of the two groups of black administrators revealed that there was no significant difference. Of all administrators, 93.8 percent responded that their ability or the institutions' ability to raise outside funds did not bear on their job security (see Table F.7).

BOOKS WRITTEN, EDITED, REVISED, OR CO-AUTHORED IN THE PAST FIVE YEARS

White administrators normally do not have the opportunity to do as much research and writing as classroom instructors, nevertheless there remains some scholarly writing by black administrators at both types of institutions. Also, when the two groups were compared, there was so significant difference on this variable (see Table F.8).

ARTICLES WRITTEN, EDITED, REVIEWED, OR CO-AUTHORED IN THE PAST FIVE YEARS

There was no significant difference between the two groups of administrators relative to this variable. A chi-square of 19.22 and a significance of 0.5072 showed that the null hypothesis is supported (see Table F.9).

BLACK STUDIES

This variable relates to involvement in black studies. A chi-square of 9.43 and a significance of 0.0090 indicated that the null hypothesis should be rejected. Black administrators at white institutions had more involvement with black studies than their counterparts at black institutions. In some instances, black administrators in lower positions at white colleges are required to be involved in black studies as a position requirement. Many of the black administrators at white institutions volunteer to take part in black studies programs and are very conscientious about maintaining the very highest quality of program output. Many black administrators at white colleges indicated that involvement in black studies programs allowed them contact with black students and black communities that might not ordinarily be possible for an administrator in the campus setting.

At black institutions, there is not the necessity for black administrators to be involved in black studies. Also, it is often stated that white students have a greater need to be exposed to the black experience than do black students. However, only 12.4 percent of all black administrators were involved with black studies. (See Table 6.6.)

THESES DIRECTED IN THE PAST FIVE YEARS

A chi-square of 13.63 and a significance of .4787 revealed that there was no significant difference between the two groups of administrators relative to this variable. Therefore, the null hypothesis was supported (see Table F.10).

DISSERTATIONS DIRECTED IN THE PAST FIVE YEARS

A comparison of the two groups of black administrators resulted in a chi-square of 5.33 and a significance of .5018. This indicated that there was no significant difference between the two groups of administrators. See Table F.11 for a complete description.

THESES COMMITTEES SERVED ON

This variable relates to the total number of theses committees that the administrators have served on. The findings supported the null hypothesis. The chi-square was 15.10, with a significance of .7160 (see Table F.12).

DISSERTATION COMMITTEES SERVED ON

The total number of dissertation committees that have been served on was not significantly different between the two groups of black administrators. The chi-square was 15.55, with a significance of .2126 (see Table F.13).

FULL TIME OR PART TIME

This variable relates to whether the respondents' administrative duties are full time or part time. When the two groups of administrators were compared, there were no significant differences between them. A chi-square of 2.58 and a significance of .1079 supported the null hypothesis (see Table G.1).

TABLE 6.6

Significance of Difference Between Black Administrators
Working at Black and White Land-Grant Institutions
of Higher Education Relating to Their
Involvement with Black Studies

Black Studies	Count Row Pc t Col Pc t Total Pc t	Type of Institution		Row Total
		Black 1	White 2	
Required	1.	3 60.0 1.7 1.0	2 40.0 1.7 .7	5 1.7
Voluntary	2.	11 34.4 6.2 3.7	21 65.6 17.4 7.0	32 10.7
Not involved with Black Studies	3.	164 62.6 92.1 54.8	98 37.4 81.0 32.8	262 87.6
Column total		178 59.5	121 40.5	299 100.0

Chi-square = 9.4734 with 2 degrees of freedom. Significance = .0090. Number of missing observations = 20.

Source: Compiled by the author.

83

LINE OR STAFF ADMINISTRATOR

The majority of black administrators at black institutions held line positions, while their counterparts at white institutions held a lesser percentage of line positions. When the two groups were compared, a chi-square of 12.82 and a significance of .0003 resulted. Table 6.7 provides more clarification.

EXERCISE OF AUTHORITY

When the two groups of black administrators were compared relative to what type of authority they exercised, there was no significant difference between them. A chi-square of 6.20 and a significance of .1021 indicated that the null hypothesis should be supported (see Table G.2). The areas of authority described were department, college or division, institution, and other. However, because 23.1 percent of the responses were in the "other" category, supplementary tables are included to provide a better picture. Therefore, Tables G.3 through G.7 give percentage breakdowns for authority exercised over other academic and administrative positions, classified staff, fiscal matters, travel within and out of state, and purchase of capital equipment.

DECISIONS REJECTED

This variable relates to the percentage of administrative decisions of the respondents that are rejected by higher authorities. The comparison of the two groups showed no significant difference between them. The chi-square of 3.84 and significance of .5732 therefore, indicated that support of the null hypothesis was appropriate. Table G.8 can be referred to for a more detailed description.

DECISIONS CARRIED OUT

This variable relates to how the two groups of administrators' decisions are carried out by their classified staffs. No significant difference was found when the two groups were compared, as reflected by a chi-square of 5.81 and a significance of .1212 (see Table G.9).

TABLE 6.7

Significance of Difference Between Black Administrators
Working at Black and White Land-Grant Institutions
of Higher Education Relating to Their Being
Line or Staff Administrators

		Type of Institution		
	Count			Row Total
	Row Pc t	Black	White	
	Col Pc t			
Line/Staff	Total Pc t	1	2	
Line	1.	136 66.3 77.3 45.8	69 33.7 57.0 23.2	205 69.0
Staff	2.	40 43.5 22.7 13.5	52 56.5 43.0 17.5	92 31.0
Column total		176 59.3	121 40.7	297 100.0

Corrected chi-square = 12.81840 with 1 degree of freedom.
Significance = .0003. Number of missing observations = 22.
Source: Compiled by the author.

SUMMARY

In summary, the hypothesis that no differences exist in the 24 variables of professional characteristics of black administrators who work at black and white institutions of higher education was supported for the following 17 variables: types of students taught; length of yearly appointment; annual salary; research and writing; administration; funding for position; jobs dependent upon; books written, edited, reviewed, or co-authored; theses directed; dissertations directed; theses committees; dissertation committees; full-time or part-time positions; exercise of authority; decisions rejected; and decisions carried out.

The hypothesis was rejected for the following seven variables: academic rank, stability of position, time in position, teaching, community service, black studies, and line or staff administrator.

Major findings were that black administrators at black institutions significantly held higher rank than their counterparts at white institutions. Black administrators at white institutions significantly held more positions that were administrative only. At black institutions, black administrators were in more stable positions than black administrators at white institutions. Significantly more black administrators at black institutions were tenured or tenure-tracked than their counterparts at white institutions. Also, black administrators at black institutions have been in their administrative positions significantly longer periods of time than their counterparts at white institutions. It was found that significantly more time is devoted to teaching by black administrators at black institutions than by their counterparts at white institutions. On the other hand, significantly more time is devoted to community service by black administrators at white institutions than by black administrators at black institutions. Black administrators at white institutions were found to be more involved with black studies than their counterparts at black institutions. Finally, black administrators at black institutions have significantly more line positions, while their counterparts at white institutions hold more staff positions.

7

DIFFERENCES IN OPINIONS AND PERCEPTIONS TOWARD EMPLOYMENT

A fourth hypothesis constructed stated that no differences exist in the six variables of opinions and perceptions toward employment by black administrators who work at black and white land-grant institutions of higher education. The chi-square test was used to determine the validity of the hypothesis for each of the six variables at the 5 percent level of significance. The results are as follows.

RACIAL DISCRIMINATION

This variable relates to perceived racial discrimination relative to the hiring of black administrators. A comparison of the two groups of black administrators resulted in a chi-square of 143.45 and a significance of 0.0000, indicating that there was a difference between the two groups of administrators.

Black administrators at white institutions perceived significantly more racial discrimination than those black administrators at black institutions. This comes in light of the fact that most public black institutions have had to integrate their faculties and administrations at a time when blacks are finding difficulty in securing administrative positions in higher education. Yet, unlike the black administrators at white institutions, black administrators at black institutions do not perceive of there being any significant amount of racial discrimination, including discrimination that might be directed toward white administrative colleagues. If white administrators at black institutions were surveyed, they might present a different picture. However, although a very interesting inquiry, the perceptions of white administrators working at black institutions are not the focus of this study. (See Table 7.1.)

TABLE 7.1

Significance of Difference Between Black Administrators
Working at Black and White Land-Grant Institutions
of Higher Education Relating to Racial
Discrimination at Their Institutions

		Type of Institution		
	Count			Row Total
	Row Pc t	Black	White	
Racial	Col Pc t			
Discrimination	Total Pc t	1	2	
None	1.	119	4	123
		96.7	3.3	42.1
		68.8	3.4	
		40.8	1.4	
Moderate	2.	35	40	75
		46.7	53.3	25.7
		20.2	33.6	
		12.0	13.7	
Prevalent	3.	9	63	72
		12.5	87.5	24.7
		5.2	52.9	
		3.1	21.6	
Don't know	4.	10	12	22
		45.5	54.5	7.5
		5.8	10.1	
		3.4	4.1	
Column total		173	119	292
		59.2	40.8	100.0

Chi-square = 143.45540 with 3 degrees of freedom. Significance = .0000. Number of missing observations = 27.

Source: Compiled by the author.

EFFORT NECESSARY FOR PROMOTION

The amount of effort perceived as being necessary for promotion in relation to white counterparts was found to be significantly different between the two groups of black administrators.

Black administrators at white institutions significantly perceived more effort being required for promotion than was required of their white counterparts. In fact, 27.3 percent of the black administrators at white institutions perceived that slightly greater effort was required for promotion. Of the black administrators at white land-grant institutions, 31.8 percent perceived that far greater effort was required for them to be promoted as compared to their white colleagues.

The majority of black administrators at black institutions perceived the effort for promotion as being the same for black and white administrators. (See Table 7.2.)

PLAN TO REMAIN AT PRESENT INSTITUTION

The length of time that the administrators plan to remain at their present institutions was significantly different between the two groups of administrators. Many black administrators at white institutions say that they only plan to remain at their present institutions for as long as it takes to find a suitable position elsewhere. Over 45 percent of the black administrators at white institutions indicate that they plan to remain at their present institutions for four more years or less.

Among the black administrators at white institutions who express the strongest desire to change institutions are those persons who hold lower positions and have the lowest seniority. The black administrators at white institutions who hold the higher level positions express little dissatisfaction with their present employment conditions.

Black administrators at black institutions plan to remain at their present institutions for longer periods of time than their black counterparts at white institutions. In some instances the decisions are influenced by the administrator nearing retirement age who would like to serve out his/her remaining career at the present black institution. Also, more black administrators at black institutions are nearing retirement age than their counterparts at white institutions. (See Table 7.3.)

PROFESSIONAL SATISFACTION

Black administrators at white institutions show significantly less professional satisfaction with their present positions than black

TABLE 7.2

Significance of Difference Between Black Administrators
Working at Black and White Land-Grant Institutions of
Higher Education Relating to the Amount of Effort
They Perceive Required for Promotion in Relation
to That of Their White Counterparts

Effort for Promotion	Count Row Pc t Col Pc t Total Pc t	Type of Institution		Row Total
		Black 1	White 2	
Far less	1.	10 90.0 8.1 4.3	1 9.1 .9 .4	11 4.7
Slightly less	2.	12 70.6 9.7 5.1	5 29.4 4.5 2.1	17 7.3
Same amount	3.	93 70.5 75.0 39.7	39 29.5 35.5 16.7	132 56.4
Slightly greater	4.	7 18.9 5.6 3.0	30 81.1 27.3 12.8	37 15.8
Far greater	5.	2 5.4 1.6 .9	35 94.6 31.8 15.0	37 15.8
Column total		124 53.0	110 47.0	234 100.0

Chi-square = 75.49927 with 4 degrees of freedom. Significance = .0000. Number of missing observations = 85.
Source: Compiled by the author.

TABLE 7.3

Significance of Difference Between Black Administrators
Working at Black and White Land-Grant Institutions of
Higher Education Relating to How Long They Plan
to Remain at Their Present Institution

| Plan to Remain (Years) | Count Row Pc t Col Pc t Total Pc t | Type of Institution | | Row Total |
		Black 1	White 2	
1	1.	13 41.9 7.1 4.3	18 58.1 14.8 5.9	31 10.2
2-4	2.	37 49.3 20.3 12.2	38 50.7 31.1 12.5	75 24.7
5 or more	3.	40 70.2 22.0 13.2	17 29.8 13.9 5.6	57 18.8
Do not know	4.	92 65.2 50.5 30.3	49 34.8 40.2 16.1	141 46.4
Column total		182 59.9	122 40.1	304 100.0

Chi-square = 11.83279 with 3 degrees of freedom. Significance = .0080. Number of missing observations = 15.

Source: Compiled by the author.

administrators at black institutions. Many of the reasons have already been enumerated relative to other variables that have been considered. However, by referring to Table 7.4, one can see that the
extent of professional dissatisfaction of black administrators at white
institutions is overwhelmingly greater than for their counterparts at
black institutions.

JOB WAS CREATED

This variable relates to whether or not the respondents perceived that their jobs were created as a result of black student and/or
affirmative action demands. A chi-square of 81.30 and a significance
of 0.0000 indicated that the null hypothesis should be rejected. The
majority of black administrators at white institutions believed that
their jobs were created as a result of black student and/or affirmative
action demands. Black administrators at black institutions did not
share the same perception. (See Table 7.5.)

DIRECT CONTACT WITH BLACK STUDENTS

There was a significant difference between the two groups of
administrators on this variable. Black administrators at black institutions showed more satisfaction with the amount of direct contact
with black students than did their black counterparts at white institutions. (See Table 7.6.)

In summarizing the findings relative to attitudes and opinions
toward present employment, there were significant differences between
the two groups of administrators on all of the six variables. Racial
discrimination was perceived more prevalent in employment at white
institutions. More effort was perceived as being necessary for black
administrators to be promoted at white institutions relative to the
amount of effort required by their white counterparts. Black administrators working at black institutions planned to remain at their institutions longer than their counterparts at white institutions. There
was more professional satisfaction with present position and future
prospects among black administrators at black institutions. The
majority of black administrators at white institutions perceived that
their jobs were created as a result of black student and/or affirmative
action demands, while their counterparts at black institutions did not
share that perception. Finally, black administrators at white institutions showed less satisfaction with the amount of direct contact with
black students.

TABLE 7.4

Significance of Difference Between Black Administrators
Working at Black and White Land-Grant Institutions
of Higher Education Relating to the Satisfaction
With Present Position and Future Prospects

Satisfied with Present Position	Count Row Pc t Col Pc t Total Pc t	Type of Institution		Row Total
		Black	White	
		1	2	
Very satisfied	1.	72 75.0 39.6 23.6	24 25.0 19.5 7.9	96 31.5
Satisfied	2.	65 57.5 35.7 21.3	48 42.5 39.0 15.7	113 37.0
Neutral	3.	24 50.0 13.2 7.9	24 50.0 19.5 7.9	48 15.7
Dissatisfied	4.	17 44.7 9.3 5.6	21 55.3 17.1 6.9	38 12.5
Greatly dissatisfied	5.	4 40.0 2.2 1.3	6 60.0 4.9 2.0	10
Column total		18 59.7	123 40.3	305 100.0

Chi-square = 16.58611 with 4 degrees of freedom. Significance =
.0023. Number of missing observations = 14.
Source: Compiled by the author.

TABLE 7.5

Significance of Difference Between Black Administrators
Working at Black and White Land-Grant Institutions
of Higher Education Relating to Their Perception
of Whether or not Their Positions Were Created
as a Result of Black Student and/or
Affirmative Action Demands

		Type of Institution		
	Count			
	Row Pc t	Black	White	Row Total
	Col Pc t			
Job Created	Total Pc t	1	2	
Yes	1.	15 17.9 8.6 5.1	69 82.1 57.5 23.4	84 28.5
No	2.	160 75.8 91.4 54.2	51 24.2 42.5 17.3	211 71.5
Column total		175 59.3	120 40.7	295 100.0

Corrected chi-square = 81.29156 with 1 degree of freedom.
Significance = .0000. Number of missing observations = 24.
Source: Compiled by the author.

94

TABLE 7.6

Significance of Difference Between Black Administrators
Working at Black and White Land-Grant Institutions
of Higher Education Relating to the Amount
of Direct Contact with Black Students

Direct Contact	Count Row Pc t Col Pc t Total Pc t	Type of Institution		Row Total
		Black	White	
		1	2	
1. Very satisfied	1.	126 74.1 72.4 43.2	44 25.9 37.3 15.1	170 58.2
Satisfied	2.	44 43.1 25.3 15.1	58 56.9 49.2 19.9	102 34.9
Dissatisfied	3.	3 20.0 1.7 1.0	12 80.0 10.2 4.1	15 5.1
Very dissatisfied	4.	1 20.0 .6 .3	4 80.0 3.4 1.4	5 1.7
Column total		174 59.6	118 40.4	292 100.0

Chi-square = 39.383330 with 3 degrees of freedom. Significance =
.0000. Number of missing observations = 27.
Source: Compiled by the author.

SUMMARY

The findings of this study are summarized as follows. No statistically significant differences exist in the fourteen variables of background characteristics of black administrators who work at black and white institutions of higher education. The null hypothesis was rejected for seven variables and supported for seven variables. No statistically significant differences exist in the seven variables of the methods of recruitment and/or selection of higher education. The null hypothesis was supported for two variables and rejected for five variable No statistically significant differences exist in the twenty-four variables of professional characteristics of black administrators who work at black and white institutions of higher education. The null hypothesis was supported for seventeen variables and rejected for seven variables. Finally, no statistically significant differences exist in the six variables of opinions and perceptions toward employment by black administrators who work at black and white institutions of higher education. The null hypothesis was rejected for all the six variables.

8

CONCLUSIONS AND
RECOMMENDATIONS

CONCLUSIONS

A number of conclusions have been reached as a result of the findings of this study. Each of the conclusions will be followed by discussions of the variables that led to it.

There are some differences relative to background characteristics of black administrators who work at black and white land-grant institutions of higher education that possibly will lead to shortages of black administrators at these institutions in the near future. In consideration of the fact that over 60 percent of all black administrators working at black land-grant institutions of higher education are over 44 years of age, the median age for all black administrators who were used for this study, it is conceivable that in the near future there will be shortages of trained black administrators to serve black land-grant institutions. Also, with the present shortages of black administrators on white land-grant campuses, these institutions will also face the dilemma of finding trained black administrators. Finding trained black higher administrators in the future is further complicated by the fact that many black scholars are presently finding it difficult to gain tenure at white land-grant institutions.

The future for black women in administration at land-grant institutions looks even poorer when one considers that they are less than 30 percent of the black administrators working at these institutions. Black women also hold lower positions than black male administrators.

With the present trends of integration in higher education, many scholars and public figures are saying that black institutions of higher education will be needed less in the future and consequently should receive diminishing levels of public revenue in the future.

However, the findings of this study show that the majority of all black administrators working at black and white land-grant institutions were raised in small cities and earned their undergraduate degrees from predominantly black institutions. Also, many black administrators who were previously working at white land-grant institutions are returning to or are seeking employment at black institutions. The trend in black student enrollment is also shifting to black institutions nationally. Therefore, while public funding is only one variable related to the overall growth and development of black institutions of higher education, it is an important determinant to the future development of more black higher educational administrators. Most black administrators have in the past and may continue in the future to receive their undergraduate degrees from black higher institutions.

It was found that over 75 percent of all black administrators working at black and white land-grant institutions of higher education received their master's degrees from white institutions. However, at black land-grant institutions, over 30 percent of the black administrators received their master's degrees from black institutions. This—combined with the facts that over 13 percent of black administrators at white land-grant institutions received their master's degrees from black institutions, the trend of black student enrollment again shifting toward black institutions, the large number of top black administrators at black land-grant institutions who are nearing retirement age, the call for less public funding for black institutions as an entity in the future, and the small number of few black administrators on white land-grant campuses—leads to the conclusion that there will be a shortage of black administrators on land-grant campuses in the near future.

While political preference is not considered to be important to the future development of black administrators in higher education, however political views of black scholars are considered an important factor when the following findings are considered: There were no significant differences in the educational level or in the types of institutions where black administrators earned their doctorates; there were no differences in the parental backgrounds between the two groups of black administrators investigated; and the differences in religious preference are not considered to be a factor in the future development of black administrators.

Political views, then, are significantly important to the future development of more black administrators at land-grant institutions. This contention is supported by the fact that 54.1 percent of black administrators at white land-grant institutions consider themselves to be "left of center" in their political views as compared to only 34.6 percent of their counterparts at black land-grant institutions. Considering that many black administrators are finding much difficulty in gaining tenure and promotions at white land-grant institutions and the possible unwillingness of black land-grant institutions to tolerate extremism, political views may be an important variable in the future development of black administrators at land-grant institutions.

There are some differences in the methods of recruitment and selection of black administrators who work at black and white land-grant institutions. The methods through which black administrators at black land-grant institutions got their present positions differed significantly in some ways from their counterparts at white land-grant institutions. Far more black administrators at black institutions learned about their present positions from friends and/or professional colleagues or were in part elevated by institution heads than were their counterparts at white institutions. This might possibly indicate stronger professional ties among black administrators at black land-grant institutions than among black administrators at white land-grant institutions. Also, there are fewer black administrators at white land-grant institutions who can influence the hiring of other black administrators. The findings of this study further show that there is considerably less recruitment of black administrators by white land-grant institutions than by black land-grant institutions.

Due to a lack of black scholars on white campuses in the past, it has been more difficult for black scholars to rise through the ranks to top administrative positions. While black land-grant institutions are doing almost twice the recruitment of black administrators than white land-grant institutions, black administrators are also seeking out black institutions for employment to a far greater extent than they are seeking out white land-grant institutions. These findings are considered to be resultant of the desire of black administrators wanting to further the cause of black education, the difficulties of gaining tenure and promotions at white land-grant institutions, and the pressures of institutional racism.

White land-grant institutions recently have slowed down their search for black administrators, as black student protest has declined and as affirmative action demands have been found to be surmountable. Past charges of brain drain have also had an effect on the recruitment of black scholars by white land-grant institutions. However, on a continuum of race versus professional qualifications, race has been found to be the most important criterion when white land-grant institutions hire black administrators. When blacks are hired into white administrations, they must not only have a black face but also must have the most impeccable professional credentials and qualifications.

While the results of this study show that black administrators have had more difficulty in getting their present positions at white land-grant institutions than they have had at black land-grant institutions, most black administrators were reluctant to answer the

questionnaire item relating to the perceived reasons for the difficulty
in getting their present positions. Only 79 out of the total 320 respondents answered this item. Therefore, the finding that there are
no significant differences between the two groups of black administrators relative to perceived reasons for the difficulty in getting their
present positions is suspect.

There are differences on 7 of the 24 variables of professional
characteristics of black administrators who work at black and white
land-grant institutions of higher education. Not only are black scholars finding difficulties in gaining employment at white land-grant institutions but they also are finding it difficult to advance to tenure and
to the rank of professor as compared to their counterparts at black
land-grant institutions. Administratively, more black scholars on
white land-grant campuses are in staff positions where they most
often hold an "assistant to" title and have little direct authority to
make important decisions. Only 12.7 percent of the black administrators on white land-grant campuses have the rank of professor as compared to 40.9 percent of black administrators on black land-grant
campuses.

It is recognized that the lack of black scholars at white land-
grant institutions until the most recent past would affect the numbers
of black administrators who have presently risen to the rank of professor and who have achieved high administrative title. However,
where stability of their positions is concerned, there seems to be
much less stability for black administrators working on white land-
grant campuses as compared to their counterparts on black land-grant
campuses. Far fewer black administrators at white land-grant institutions are on a tenure track than their counterparts at black land-
grant institutions. This fact cannot be explained away by citing that
blacks were not around until most recently. Nor can job market conditions be called upon to justify disparate future advancement opportunities for black administrators who are presently working at white
land-grant institutions of higher education. The fact is that future
opportunities for black administrators working at white land-grant
institutions seem much less than for black administrators working on
black land-grant campuses.

Due to differences in budgetary constraints and some differences in institutional structure, black administrators at black land-
grant institutions often must wear many hats. That is, they often
have multiple assignments and additional teaching duties. Black administrators at white land-grant institutions do not have to spread
themselves as thin. In fact, black administrators at white land-grant
institutions do much less teaching than their counterparts at black
land-grant institutions. However, black administrators at white land-
grant institutions devote much more time to community service,

partly because community service along with research and writing and teaching is stressed more at major institutions as a prerequisite for tenure and/or promotion. Also, black land-grant institutions traditionally have not had as much resource for extension services as have white land-grant institutions.

It is conceivable that at black land-grant institutions less emphasis would be placed on formal programs of black studies than at white land-grant institutions. Therefore, if black administrators at white land-grant institutions are not normally required to do much teaching and want to participate in black studies programs, it would usually be on a voluntary basis (provided they were not hired in the area of black studies). Therefore, a significant difference between the two groups of black administrators relative to their involvement in black studies is no surprise.

As has been previously mentioned, over twice as many administrators at white land-grant institutions are in staff positions as their counterparts at black land-grant institutions. Judging from responses to the questionnaire, many of the administrators on white land-grant campuses feel that their primary function is that of "institutional firemen" to solve problems related to race, keep black students in line, and to answer criticisms against their institutions in the area of race relations.

There are differences in the attitudes and opinions toward present employment between the two groups of black administrators.

Most black administrators at white land-grant institutions consider racial discrimination to be prevalent. Conversely, their black counterparts at black land-grant institutions mostly consider racial discrimination to be nonexistent. Considering the fact that at black land-grant institutions the faculties and staffs are integrated to a greater degree than the faculties and staffs of white land-grant institutions, an assumption is made that white scholars at black institutions can rise much faster than black scholars at white institutions. However, black administrators at white land-grant institutions are finding that they must work much harder to be promoted than their white colleagues at the same institutions.

It appears that the combination of institutional racism, the higher standards required for black administrators to be promoted as compared to their white colleagues, and poor relationships is causing many black administrators at white land-grant institutions to consider leaving their present institutions within the next few years. In fact, approximately 60 percent of the black administrators at white land-grant institutions plan to leave their present institutions within the next five years.

Most black administrators at black land-grant institutions plan to remain at their present institutions for far longer periods of time than their black counterparts at white institutions. Many of the black administrators at black land-grant institutions express that they are nearing retirement and will remain at their institutions until then. Others state that they would only leave their present black institution if they received an offer they couldn't refuse.

As a result of some factors mentioned above, black administrators at white land-grant institutions express significantly less professional satisfaction with their present positions than black administrators at black land-grant institutions.

Over half of the black administrators at white land-grant institutions responded that they perceived their positions as having been created as a result of black student and/or affirmative action demands. Less than 10 percent of black administrators at black land-grant institutions shared the same perception.

Black administrators on white land-grant campuses also responded that they were less satisfied with the amount of direct contact that they have with black students as compared to black administrators on black land-grant campuses. This, then, would raise the question: If over half of the black administrators on white land-grant campuses feel that their positions were created as a result of black student and/ or affirmative action demands, and these same black administrators devote more time to community service than their counterparts at black land-grant institutions, why, then, are they less satisfied with the amount of direct contact with black students? The answer must likely be that at black land-grant institutions the student bodies are predominantly black and therefore black administrators have many opportunities for direct contact with black students, on the campus and in the classroom. Conversely, black student populations on white land-grant campuses are small, diversified, and transitory. Therefore, black administrators do not have much classroom or campus exposure to black students. Also, many black students feel that white students would profit more from black studies than black students and therefore do not feel obligated to take black studies courses. This further lessens the opportunities for direct contact with black administrators who have volunteered to participate in black studies programs.

Relative to the Assumptions of This Study

Black scholars can be attracted to higher educational administration: the findings of this study support this assumption. Of all black administrators working presently at black and white land-grant institutions, 51.9 percent were recruited. Over 28 percent of all black administrators at black and white land-grant institutions applied for position vacancies.

Black scholars have not priced themselves out of the academic marketplace: the finding of this study supports this assumption. There is no significant difference in salaries between black administrators working at black and white land-grant institutions. The average salaries for black administrators working at black and white land-grant institutions are slightly below the salaries of their white counterparts.

Major institutions have aborted their efforts to locate and hire black Ph.D.s: the findings of this study support this assumption. Black administrators at white land-grant institutions are finding much difficulty in getting employment at white land-grant institutions. There is also much difficulty experienced in getting promotions and tenure. Racial discrimination is found to be prevalent by over half of black administrators working at white land-grant institutions. Amount of effort required for promotion is perceived to be much greater for black administrators as compared to their white colleagues at white land-grant institutions. Black administrators at white land-grant institutions express much less professional satisfaction than their counterparts at black land-grant institutions and plan to remain at their present white institutions for much shorter periods of time than their counterparts at black land-grant institutions.

RECOMMENDATIONS

More research should be directed to the area of black administrators in higher education relative to trends and employment possibilities, social climates within various types of higher institutions (that is, public and private), and the possibilities for tenure and/or promotion. More resources should be committed by major institutions and state and federal agencies for the development of black higher educational administrators. There should be a commitment to more employment opportunities for black administrators by major institutions of higher education. Opportunities for tenure and/or promotion of black administrators should be made equitable by major institutions. Major institutions should make more opportunities available for black administrators in all areas of their administrations exclusive of minority affairs and related staff positions. There should be a reaffirmation to equal opportunity employment to major institutions.

This study was undertaken as a result of concern about opportunities in higher education for black administrators and to bring some objective evidence to bear on the problem. Sufficient evidence was found to substantiate those concerns. The black population in the United States is presently more than 30 million people and is increasing at a higher percentage rate than the majority population. Therefore, it is conceivable that black students in increasing numbers will be entering college in the near future, thus creating more need for black administrators on both black and white campuses. Action is needed now if we are to allay a shortage of black administrators in the near future and beyond.

APPENDIX A

March 31, 1977

Dear Colleague:

I am a Ph.D. candidate in the Urban Education doctoral program at the University of Wisconsin-Milwaukee. As a dissertation study, I have elected to research the background characteristics and selected perceptions of black administrators like us working in black and white Land-Grant institutions of higher education. This study comes at a time when the atmosphere of student protest on campuses around the nation is relatively non-volatile and therefore would give a more accurate indication of the total career potential of black administrators working in white institutions of higher education as contrasted to black administrators who work in black higher institutions. Therefore, I would very much appreciate your assistance in providing the data requested.

After contacting many black scholars around the nation, I have found that this project generates much interest and concern for the future outlook of black administrators in higher education. Therefore, will you please fill out this questionnaire and return it in the enclosed self-addressed, stamped envelope as soon as possible.

All replies will be held in strict confidence and no publication derived from the information given will bear the names of individuals. All tabulations will be in numerical form. The coding on the questionnaire will be used for follow-up mailing only.

Thanks and my appreciation in advance.

Very sincerely,

Robert L. Hoskins

RLH:js
Enclosure

107

APPENDIX B

SURVEY

Black Administrators in Higher Education

Robert Hoskins

The purpose of this questionnaire is to explore differences in the academic preparation and background variables of black administrators working at a diverse set of institutions of higher education.

All information given on this questionnaire will be kept confidential and no person or persons will be identified in any report that results from this survey. The code numbers on each copy of the questionnaire will be used only for follow-up purposes, if necessary.

PLEASE CIRCLE OR SUPPLY THE APPROPRIATE
NUMBER IN ANSWER TO EACH QUESTION.

If there are any questions regarding this instrument or items that appear therein, please contact: Robert L. Hoskins, 4576 S. 20th St., Milwaukee, WI 53221, (414) 282-0942.

DEMOGRAPHIC DATA

1. Age:
   1. Less than 25
   2. 25 - 29
   3. 30 - 34
   4. 35 - 39
   5. 40 - 44
   6. 45 - 49
   7. 50 - 54
   8. 55 - 59
   9. 60 - 64
   10. 65 and over

2. Sex:
   1. Male
   2. Female

3. Size of city of upbringing (most time lived in before 18 years of age.)
   1. Under 25,000
   2. 25,000 - 49,000
   3. 50,000 - 99,000
   4. 100,000 - 499,000
   5. 500,000 - 999,000
   6. 1,000,000 and over

4. Your highest educational level:
   1. No formal degree
   2. Associate degree
   3. B.S. or B.A.
   4. Master's degree
   5. Ed.S.
   6. M.D., D.D.S., or J.D.
   7. Ed.D. or Ph.D.
   8. Other (please specify) _____

5. Was your undergraduate degree from a predominantly white or predominantly black college or university?
   1. Predominantly white   2. Predominantly black

6. Was your graduate degree(s) from a predominantly white or predominantly black college or university?

   ### Master's degree
   1. Predominantly white   2. Predominantly black

   ### Ph.D. (or other terminal degree)
   1. Predominantly white   2. Predominantly black

7. Father's <u>highest</u> educational level:
   1. Less than High School
   2. High School Graduate
   3. Associate degree
   4. B.S. or B.A.
   5. Master's degree
   6. Ed.S.
   7. M.D., D.D.S., or J.D.
   8. Ed.D. or Ph.D.
   9. Other (please specify)_____

8. Mother's <u>highest</u> educational level:
   1. No formal degree
   2. Associate degree
   3. B.S., B.A., or R.N.
   4. Master's degree
   5. Ed.S.
   6. M.D., D.D.S., or J.D.
   7. Ed.D. or Ph.D.
   8. Other (please specify)_____

9. Occupational level of <u>Father</u>:
   1. Laborer, Domestic, etc.
   2. Semi-skilled
   3. Skilled
   4. Semi-professional (Foreman, Salesman, etc.)
   5. Professional
   6. Other (please specify)_____

10. Occupational level of <u>Mother</u>:
   1. Laborer, Domestic, etc.
   2. Semi-skilled
   3. Skilled
   4. Semi-professional (L.P.N., Teachers aid, etc.)
   5. Professional
   6. Other (please specify)_____

11. Your political preference:
   1. Democrat
   2. Republican
   3. Independent
   4. Other

12. At the present time, how do you characterize your political views?
   1. Extreme left
   2. Left of center (liberal)
   3. Moderate
   4. Right of center (conservative)
   5. Extreme right
   6. Other (please specify)_____

13. Your religious preference:
    1. Protestant
    2. Roman Catholic
    3. Jewish
    4. Black Muslim
    5. Other (please specify) _____

METHODS OF RECRUITMENT AND/OR SELECTION BY WHICH YOU OBTAINED YOUR PRESENT ADMINISTRATIVE POSITION

14. How did you get your position?
    1. I was recruited.
    2. I applied for the position vacancy.
    3. I made a general application to this and other institutions.
    4. Other (please specify) _____

15. If you were employed at a predominantly black institution, what was your reason for leaving to take your present position?
    1. I was recruited for my present position.
    2. I sought my present position.
    3. I did not come to my present position from a predominantly black institution.
    4. Other (please specify) _____

16. From what source did you learn about your present position?
    1. Graduate degree advisor
    2. Graduate School
    3. Friend or professional colleague
    4. Newspaper want ads
    5. University placement service
    6. Private employment agency
    7. Mass letter or announcement
    8. Other (please specify) _____

17. In your perception, what relationship did the race vs. professional qualifications issue have in the decision to hire you or not to hire you?

    Race vs. Professional Qualification

    1. 90% ----------------------- 10%
    2. 70% ----------------------- 30%
    3. 50% ----------------------- 50%
    4. 30% ----------------------- 70%
    5. 10% ----------------------- 90%

18. How much difficulty did you have in getting your present position?
    1. Great difficulty
    2. Some difficulty
    3. Little or no difficulty

19. If you mostly had difficulty in obtaining your present position, do you think that it was due to one of the following?
    1. General job market conditions for people in your field who have your qualifications
    2. Your requirements for accepting the position
    3. Your race
    4. Your sex
    5. Institution from which you graduated
    6. Other (please specify) _____

20. Are you in a new position or are you filling a vacancy?
    1. New position
    2. Filling a vacancy
    3. Do not know

PROFESSIONAL CHARACTERISTICS

21. What is your academic rank?
    1. Professor
    2. Associate professor
    3. Assistant professor
    4. Instructor (non-tenured)
    5. Administrative appointment only
    6. Other (please specify)_____

22. Stability of your position:
    1. Tenured
    2. Tenure tracked
    3. Not tenure tracked

23. The students you teach are:
    1. Undergraduates only
    2. Graduates only
    3. Graduates and undergraduates
    4. I have no teaching assignments

24. Length of yearly appointment:
    1. Academic year (9 mos.)
    2. Calendar year (12 mos.)

25. What is your annual salary?
    1. Less than $15,000
    2. $15,000 - $17,499
    3. $17,500 - $19,999
    4. $20,000 - $22,499
    5. $22,500 - $24,999
    6. $25,000 - $29,999
    7. $30,000 - $34,999
    8. $35,000 or above

26. How long have you held your present position?
    1. 0 - 3 years
    2. 4 - 6 years
    3. 7 - 9 years
    4. 10 - 12 years
    5. 13 - 15 years
    6. Over 15 years

28. What percent of your time is devoted to research and writing?
    1. 0 - 9%
    2. 10 - 19%
    3. 20 - 29%
    4. 30 - 39%
    5. 40 - 49%
    6. 50 - 59%
    7. 60 - 69%
    8. 70 - 79%
    9. 80 - 89%
    10. 90 - 100%

29. What percent of your time is devoted to teaching?
    1. 0 - 9%
    2. 10 - 19%
    3. 20 - 29%
    4. 30 - 39%
    5. 40 - 49%
    6. 50 - 59%
    7. 60 - 69%
    8. 70 - 79%
    9. 80 - 89%
    10. 90 - 100%

30. What percent of your time is devoted to administration?
    1. 0 - 9%
    2. 10 - 19%
    3. 20 - 29%
    4. 30 - 39%
    5. 40 - 49%
    6. 50 - 59%
    7. 60 - 69%
    8. 70 - 79%
    9. 80 - 89%
    10. 90 - 100%

31. What percent of your time is devoted to community service?
    1. 0 - 9%
    2. 10 - 19%
    3. 20 - 29%
    4. 30 - 39%
    5. 40 - 49%
    6. 50 - 59%
    7. 60 - 69%
    8. 70 - 79%
    9. 80 - 89%
    10. 90 - 100%

32. Is your position funded from special project funds from outside
    the institution or from the institution's own funds?
    1. Outside funds
    2. The institution's own funds

33. Which one of the following does the continuation of your job de-
    pend upon?
    1. Your ability to raise outside funds
    2. The institution's ability to raise outside funds
    3. Neither

34. How many published books have you written, edited, reviewed,
    or co-authored in the past five years?
        Number _____

35. How many articles have you written, edited, reviewed, or co-authored in the past five years?
    Number _____

36. Are you involved in black studies?
    1. Yes - required   3. No
    2. Yes - voluntarily

37. How many theses have you directed in the past _five_ years?
    Number _____

38. How many dissertations have you directed in the past _five_ years?
    Number _____

39. How many committees involved with theses have you served on?
    Number _____

40. How many committees involved with dissertations have you served on?
    Number _____

41. Are you a full-time or part-time administrator?
    1. Full-time   2. Part-time

42. Are you a line or staff administrator?
    1. Line   2. Staff

43. If you are a line administrator, over which of the following do you exercise authority?
    1. Department   3. Institution
    2. College or division   4. Other (please specify) _____

44. Do you have direct authority to make decisions concerning the following areas?
    1. Other academic and administrative positions
    2. Classified staff
    3. Fiscal matters related to your position
    4. Travel within and out of state
    5. Purchase of capital equipment

45. Approximately what percent of your decisions are rejected or altered by your superiors?
    1. 0 - 5%   4. 16 - 20%
    2. 6 - 10%   5. 21 - 25%
    3. 11 - 15%   6. 26 - 30%

46. Generally speaking, are your decisions <u>readily</u> carried out by your <u>classified</u> staff?
    1. Readily carried out
    2. Carried out completely, with some hesitation
    3. Partially carried out with delays
    4. Other (please specify) _____

ATTITUDES AND OPINIONS TOWARD PRESENT EMPLOYMENT

47. Relative to hiring black faculty and administrators, racial discrimination at your institution is:
    1. Non-existent   3. Prevalent
    2. Moderately existent   4. Do not know

48. How much effort is necessary for you to be promoted, in relation to your white colleagues?
    1. Far less effort than your white colleagues
    2. Slightly less effort than your white colleagues
    3. The same amount of effort as your white colleagues
    4. Slightly greater effort than your white colleagues
    5. Far greater effort than your white colleagues

49. How long do you plan to remain at your present institution?
    1. Another 1 year   3. 5 years or more
    2. Another 2 - 4 years   4. Do not know

50. Are you professionally satisfied with your present position and its future prospects?
    1. Very satisfied   4. Dissatisfied
    2. Satisfied   5. Greatly dissatisfied
    3. Neutral

51. Do you believe that your job was created as a result of black student and/or affirmative action demands?
    1. Yes   2. No

52. The amount of direct contact I have with black students is:
    1. Very satisfactory   3. Unsatisfactory
    2. Satisfactory   4. Very unsatisfactory

APPENDIX C

TABLE C.1

State-Supported Large White Institutions of Higher Education—5,000
or More Students, Graduate and Undergraduate,
Who Are Working for a Degree (Spring 1976)

Name	Location	Number of Students
University of Akron	Akron, Ohio 44325	21,757
University of Alabama	University, Ala. 35486	15,774
University of Alabama	Birmingham, Ala. 35294	11,019
University of Alaska	Anchorage, Alaska 99504	7,281
University of Arizona	Tucson, Ariz. 85721	28,971
State University of Arizona	Tempe, Ariz. 85281	33,346
University of Arkansas	Fayetteville, Ark. 72701	12,250
University of Arkansas	Little Rock, Ark. 72204	8,500
Arkansas State University	State University, Ark. 72467	6,541
Auburn University	Auburn, Ala. 36830	5,332
Ball State University	Muncie, Ind. 47306	15,884
University of Baltimore	Baltimore, Md. 21201	5,800
Bloomsburg State College	Bloomsburg, Pa. 17815	5,711
Boise State University	Boise, Idaho 83725	11,500
Boston State College	Boston, Mass. 02115	5,530
Bowling Green State University	Bowling Green, Ohio 43403	16,412
University of California, Berkeley	Berkeley, California 94720	28,298

(continued)

(Table C.1   continued)

Name	Location	Number of Students
University of California, Davis	Davis, California 95616	16,950
University of California, Irvine	Irvine, California 92717	8,622
University of California, Los Angeles	Los Angeles, California 90024	31,735
University of California, Riverside	Riverside, California 92502	5,129
University of California, San Diego	LaJolla, California 92093	9,438
University of California, Santa Barbara	Santa Barbara, California 93106	14,178
University of California, Santa Cruz	Santa Cruz, California 95064	6,105
California Polytech State University	San Luis Obispo, California 93407	14,508
California State College	California, Pa. 15419	5,075
California State College	Dominquez Hills, California 90747	6,600
California State College, Sonoma	Rohnert Park, California 94928	5,900
California State Polytech University	Pomona, California 91768	12,651
California State University, Chico	Chico, California 95926	12,920
California State University, Fresno	Fresno, California 93740	15,300

(Table C.1   continued)

Name	Location	Number of Students
California State University, Fullerton	Fullerton, California 92634	21,700
California State University, Hayward	Hayward, California 94542	11,205
California State University, Long Beach	Long Beach, California 90840	31,700
California State University, Los Angeles	Los Angeles, California 90032	25,500
California State University, Northridge	Northridge, California 91330	27,778
California State University, Sacramento	Sacramento, California 95819	20,808
Cameron University	Lawton, Okla. 73501	6,000
Central Connecticut State College	New Britain, Conn. 06050	8,027
Central Michigan University	Mt. Pleasant, Mich. 48859	14,836
Central Missouri State University	Warrensburg, Mo. 64093	9,678
Central State University	Edmond, Okla. 73034	11,250
Central Washington State College	Ellensburg, Wash. 98926	8,000
College of Charleston	Charleston, S.C. 29401	5,397
University of Cincinnati	Cincinnati, Ohio 45221	32,000
Clemson University	Clemson, S.C. 29631	10,970
Cleveland State University	Cleveland, Ohio 44115	16,974

(continued)

(Table C.1   continued)

Name	Location	Number of Students
University of Colorado	Boulder, Colo. 80302	22,430
University of Colorado Denver	Denver, Colo. 80202	8,097
Colorado State University	Fort Collins, Colo. 80523	15,867
Columbus College	Columbus, Ga. 31907	5,497
University of Connecticut	Storrs, Conn. 06268	22,025
East Tennessee State University	Johnson City, Tenn. 37601	9,244
East Texas State University	Commerce, Tex. 75428	8,982
Eastern Illinois University	Charleston, Ill. 61920	8,994
Eastern Kentucky University	Richmond, Ky. 40475	13,430
Eastern Michigan University	Ypsilanti, Mich. 48197	17,704
Eastern Washington State College	Cheney, Wash. 99004	6,305
Edinboro State College	Edinboro, Pa. 16444	7,041
Emporia Kansas State College	Emporia, Kans. 66801	5,888
Fairmont State College	Fairmont, W. Va. 26554	5,078
Ferris State College	Big Rapids, Mich. 49307	8,608
University of Florida	Gainesville, Fla. 32611	28,189
Florida Atlantic University	Boca Raton, Florida 33421	6,846

(Table C.1   continued)

Name	Location	Number of Students
Florida International University	Miami, Fla. 33195	11,000
Florida State University	Tallahassee, Fla. 32306	19,128
Florida Technical University	Orlando, Fla. 32876	10,641
George Mason University	Fairfax, Va. 22030	7,843
University of Georgia	Athens, Ga. 30602	21,442
Georgia Institute of Technology	Atlanta, Ga. 30332	7,815
Georgia Southern College	Statesboro, Ga. 30958	5,400
Georgia State University	Atlanta, Ga. 30303	21,075
Glassboro State College	Glassboro, N.J. 08028	11,674
Grand Valley State College	Allendale, Mich. 49901	6,803
University of Hawaii, Manoa	Honolulu, Hawaii 96822	20,397
University of Houston	Houston, Tex. 77004	28,714
Humboldt State University	Arcata, Calif. 95521	7,706
University of Idaho	Moscow, Idaho 83843	8,134
Idaho State University	Pocatello, Idaho 83201	9,412
University of Illinois, Chicago Circle	Chicago, Ill. 60680	19,519
University of Illinois, Urbana-Champaign	Urbana, Ill. 61801	32,823

(continued)

(Table C.1   continued)

Name	Location	Number of Students
Illinois State University	Normal, Ill. 61761	19,000
Indiana State University	Terre Haute, Ind. 47809	10,531
Indiana University	Bloomington, Ind. 47407	32,651
Indiana University–Purdue University	Fort Wayne, Ind. 46805	8,418
Indiana University–Purdue University	Indianapolis, Ind. 46202	20,131
Indiana University	South Bend, Ind. 46616	5,771
Indiana University of Pennsylvania	Indiana, Pa. 15701	10,873
University of Iowa	Iowa City, Iowa 52240	21,134
Iowa State University	Ames, Iowa 50011	21,205
Jacksonville State University	Jacksonville, Fla. 36265	6,400
Jersey City State College	Jersey City, N.J. 07305	11,603
University of Kansas	Lawrence, Kan. 66045	23,541
Kansas State College	Pittsburg, Kan. 66762	5,688
Kansas State University	Manhattan, Kan. 66506	17,901
Kean College of New Jersey	Union, N.J. 07083	13,600
Kearny State College	Kearny, Neb. 68847	5,234
Kent State University	Kent, Ohio 44242	26,800
University of Kentucky	Lexington, Ky. 40502	18,845

(Table C.1   continued)

Name	Location	Number of Students
Kutztown State College	Kutztown, Pa. 19530	5,143
Lamar University	Beaumont, Tex. 77710	12,156
Louisiana State University, Baton Rouge	Baton Rouge, La. 71270	22,693
Louisiana Technical University	Ruston, La. 70803	8,174
University of Louisville	Louisville, Ky. 40208	15,787
University of Lowell	Lowell, Mass. 01854	8,000
Madison College	Harrisonburg, Va. 22801	7,071
University of Maine, Orono	Orono, Maine 04473	10,513
University of Maine, Portland-Gorham	Portland, Maine 04103	6,800
Marshall University	Huntington, W. Va. 25701	10,367
University of Maryland	Catonsville, Md. 21228	5,600
University of Maryland	College Park, Md. 20742	33,803
University of Maryland University College	College Park, Md. 20742	12,455
University of Massachusetts, Amherst	Amherst, Mass. 01002	24,772
University of Massachusetts, Boston	Boston, Mass. 02125	7,380
McNeese State University	Lake Charles, La. 70601	5,720
Memphis State University	Memphis, Tenn. 38152	21,305

(continued)

(Table C.1   continued)

Name	Location	Number of Students
Metropolitan State College	Denver, Colo. 80204	12,500
Miami University	Oxford, Ohio 45056	14,390
University of Michigan	East Lansing, Mich. 48824	40,808
Michigan State University	Ann Arbor, Mich. 48104	37,505
Michigan Technical University	Houghton, Mich. 49931	5,481
Middle Tennessee State University	Murpreesboro, Tenn. 37132	9,701
Millersville State College	Millersville, Pa. 17557	6,179
University of Minnesota	Minneapolis-St. Paul, Minn. 55455	70,000
University of Minnesota	Duluth, Minn. 55812	5,500
Mankato State University	Mankato, Minn. 56001	13,616
Moorhead State University	Moorhead, Minn. 56560	6,374
St. Cloud State University	St. Cloud, Minn. 56258	10,118
University of Mississippi	University, Miss. 38677	8,500
Mississippi State University	Starkville, Miss. 39762	11,709
University of Missouri	Columbia, Mo. 65201	23,400
University of Missouri	Kansas City, Mo. 64110	11,400
University of Missouri	St. Louis, Mo. 63121	11,850
University of Montana	Missoula, Mont. 59801	8,693

(Table C.1   continued)

Name	Location	Number of Students
Montana State University	Bozeman, Mont. 59715	8,002
Montclair State College	Upper Montclair, N.J. 07043	15,107
Morehead State University	Morehead, Ky. 40357	7,318
Murray State University	Murray, Ky. 42071	8,232
University of Nebraska	Lincoln, Neb. 68508	20,892
University of Nebraska	Omaha, Neb. 68101	14,294
University of Nevada	Reno, Nev. 89507	8,225
University of Nevada	Las Vegas, Nev. 89154	8,382
University of New Hampshire	Durham, N.H. 03824	9,800
University of New Mexico	Albuquerque, N. Mex. 87131	20,032
New Mexico State University	Las Cruces, N. Mex. 88001	10,092
University of New Orleans	New Orleans, La. 70122	13,031
State University of New York, Albany	Albany, N.Y. 12222	14,750
State University of New York, Binghamton	Binghamton, N.Y. 13901	9,693
State University of New York, Buffalo	Buffalo, N.Y. 14214	24,971
State University of New York, Stony Brook	Stony Brook, N.Y. 11794	15,713

(continued)

(Table C.1   continued)

Name	Location	Number of Students
State University of New York College, Brockport	Brockport, N.Y. 14420	11,103
State University of New York College, Buffalo	Buffalo, N.Y. 14222	12,087
State University of New York College, Cortland	Cortland, N.Y. 13045	5,665
State University of New York College, Geneseo	Geneseo, N.Y. 14454	6,031
State University of New York College, New Paltz	New Paltz, N.Y. 12561	8,892
State University of New York College, Oneonta	Oneonta, N.Y. 13820	6,253
State University of New York College, Oswego	Oswego, N.Y. 13121	9,143
State University of New York College, Plattsburgh	Plattsburgh, N.Y. 12901	6,181
Nichols State University	Thibodaux, La. 70301	6,066
Norfolk State College	Norfolk, Va. 23504	6,827
Appalachian State University	Boone, N.C. 28608	9,945
East Carolina University	Greenville, N.C. 27834	11,015
North Carolina State University	Raleigh, N.C. 27607	16,542
University of North Carolina	Chapel Hill, N.C. 27514	19,370

(Table C.1   continued)

Name	Location	Number of Students
University of North Carolina	Charlotte, N.C. 28223	7,252
University of North Carolina	Greensboro, N.C. 27412	9,155
Western Carolina University	Cullowhee, N.C. 28723	6,084
University of North Dakota	Grand Forks, N. Dak. 58202	8,632
North Dakota State University	Fargo, N. Dak. 58102	6,957
North Texas State University	Denton, Tex. 76203	15,607
Northeast Louisiana University	Monroe, La. 71201	9,040
Northeast Missouri State University	Kirksville, Mo. 63501	5,500
Northeastern Illinois University	Chicago, Ill. 60625	9,492
Northeastern Oklahoma State University	Tahlequah, Okla. 74464	5,763
Northern Arizona University	Flagstaff, Ariz. 86001	10,956
Northern Colorado University	Greeley, Colo. 80639	9,655
Northern Illinois University	Dekalb, Ill. 60115	20,117

(continued)

(Table C.1   continued)

Name	Location	Number of Students
University of Northern Iowa	Cedar Falls, Iowa 50613	8,676
Northern Kentucky University	Highland Heights, Ky. 41076	5,618
Northern Michigan University	Marquette, Mich. 49885	8,800
Northwestern State University of Louisiana	Natchitoches, La. 71457	6,685
Ohio State University	Columbus, Ohio 43210	46,817
Ohio University	Athens, Ohio 45701	15,140
University of Oklahoma	Norman, Okla. 73069	19,799
Oklahoma State University	Stillwater, Okla. 74074	18,009
Old Dominion University	Norfolk, Va. 23508	13,160
University of Oregon	Eugene, Ore. 97403	15,488
Oregon State University	Corvallis, Ore. 97331	16,188
Pan American University	Edinburg, Tex. 78539	8,249
Pennsylvania State University	University Park, Pa. 16802	70,767
Portland State University	Portland, Ore. 97207	13,500
University of Puerto Rico	Rio Piedras, Puerto Rico 00931	25,719
University of Puerto Rico	Mayaquez, Puerto Rico 00708	9,334
Purdue University	West Lafayette, Ind. 47907	27,768

(Table C.1   continued)

Name	Location	Number of Students
Purdue University	Hammond, Ind. 46323	6,478
University of Rhode Island	Kingston, R.I. 02908	8,714
Rutgers University	New Brunswick, N. J. 08903	46,305
Sam Houston State University	Huntsville, Tex. 77340	9,864
San Diego State University	San Diego, Calif. 92182	30,121
San Francisco State University	San Francisco, Calif. 94132	25,000
San Jose State University	San Jose, Calif. 95192	27,000
Shippensburg State College	Shippensburg, Pa. 17257	5,506
Slippery Rock State College	Slippery Rock, Pa. 16057	5,815
University of South Alabama	Mobile, Ala. 36688	6,067
University of South Carolina	Columbia, S.C. 29208	29,378
University of South Dakota	Vermillion, S. Dak. 57069	5,450
South Dakota State University	Brookings, S. Dak. 57006	6,412
University of South Florida	Tampa, Fla. 33620	21,196
Southeast Missouri State University	Cape Girardeau, Mo. 63701	7,550
Southeastern Louisiana University	Hammond, La. 70401	6,700

(continued)

(Table C.1   continued)

Name	Location	Number of Students
University of Southern Colorado	Pueblo, Colo. 81001	6,000
Southern Connecticut State College	New Haven, Conn. 06515	12,497
Southern Illinois University	Carbondale, Ill. 62901	21,000
Southern Illinois University	Edwardsville, Ill. 62025	12,212
University of Southern Mississippi	Hattiesburg, Miss. 39401	11,404
Southwest Missouri State University	Springfield, Mo. 65802	11,000
Southwest Texas State University	San Marcos, Tex. 78666	13,011
University of Southwestern Louisiana	Lafayette, La. 70501	12,329
Stephen F. Austin State University	Nacogdoches, Tex. 75961	10,225
University of Tennessee	Chattanooga, Tenn. 37401	5,808
University of Tennessee	Knoxville, Tenn. 37916	29,999
University of Tennessee	Martin, Tenn. 38238	5,188
University of Tennessee	Nashville, Tenn. 37203	5,493
Tennessee Technical University	Cookesville, Tenn. 38501	7,120
Texas A&I University	Kingsville, Tex. 78363	7,441
Texas A&M University	College Station, Tex. 77843	24,293

(Table C.1   continued)

Name	Location	Number of Students
University of Texas	Arlington, Tex. 76019	16,000
University of Texas	Austin, Tex. 78712	42,598
University of Texas	El Paso, Tex. 79963	13,600
Texas Technical University	Lubbock, Tex. 79401	20,820
Texas Women's University	Denton, Tex. 76204	8,086
University of Toledo	Toledo, Ohio 43606	14,953
Towson State College	Towson, Md. 21204	13,838
Trenton State College	Trenton, N.J. 08625	7,000
Troy State University	Troy, Ala. 36081	10,136
University of Utah	Salt Lake City, Utah 34112	23,500
Utah State University	Logan, Utah 84322	8,926
Valdosta State College	Valdosta, Ga. 31601	5,012
University of Vermont	Burlington, Vt. 05482	8,287
University of Virginia	Charlottesville, Va. 22903	14,933
Virginia Commonwealth University	Richmond, Va. 23284	17,988
Virginia Polytechnical and State University	Blacksburg, Va. 24060	18,477
University of Washington	Seattle, Wash. 98195	35,434
Washington State University	Pullman, Wash. 99163	15,637
Wayne State University	Detroit, Mich. 48202	34,323

(continued)

(Table C.1   continued)

Name	Location	Number of Students
Weber State College	Ogden, Utah 84408	9,458
West Chester State College	West Chester, Pa. 19380	6,000
University of West Florida	Pensacola, Fla. 32504	5,231
West Georgia College	Carrollton, Ga. 30117	5,464
West Texas State University	Canyon, Tex. 79016	6,701
West Virginia University	Morgantown, W. Va. 26506	16,500
Western Illinois University	Macomb, Ill. 61455	14,000
Western Kentucky University	Bowling Green, Ky. 42101	13,040
Western Michigan University	Kalamazoo, Mich. 49008	19,914
Western Washington State College	Bellingham, Wash. 98225	8,840
Wichita State University	Wichita, Kan. 67208	14,231
William & Mary College	Williamsburg, Va. 23185	5,947

(Table C.1   continued)

Name	Location	Number of Students
William Patterson College	Wayne, N.J. 07470	13,204
University of Wisconsin	Eau Claire, Wis. 54701	9,359
University of Wisconsin	La Crosse, Wis. 54601	7,163
University of Wisconsin	Madison, Wis. 53706	38,545
University of Wisconsin	Milwaukee, Wis. 53211	23,596
University of Wisconsin	Oshkosh, Wis. 54901	10,600
University of Wisconsin, Parkside	Kenosha, Wis. 53140	5,400
University of Wisconsin	Stevens Point, Wis. 54481	8,220
University of Wisconsin, Stout	Menominee, Wis. 54751	5,600
University of Wisconsin	Whitewater, Wis. 53190	8,200
Wright State University	Dayton, Ohio 45431	12,500
University of Wyoming	Laramie, Wyo. 82071	8,078
Youngstown State University	Youngstown, Ohio	14,264

Source: Information Please Almanac (New York, 1977).

TABLE C.2

State-Supported Black Institutions of Higher Education

Name	Location	Number of Students
Alabama A&M University	Normal, Ala. 35762	4,470
Alabama State University	Montgomery, Ala. 36101	3,523
Albany State College	Albany, Ga. 31705	1,958
Alcorn State University	Lorman, Miss. 39096	2,719
University of Arkansas	Pine Bluffs, Ark.	2,556
Bluefield State College	Bluefield, W. Va. 24701	1,525
Bowie State College	Bowie, Md. 20715	3,098
Central State University	Wilberforce, Ohio 45384	2,086
Cheyney State College	Cheyney, Pa. 19319	2,750
Chicago State University	Chicago, Ill. 60628	6,633
Coppin State College	Baltimore, Md. 21216	2,359
Delaware State College	Dover, Del. 19901	2,150
Florida A&M University	Tallahassee, Fla. 33421	5,600
Fort Valley State College	Fort Valley, Ga. 31031	1,862
Grambling State University	Grambling, La. 71245	3,749
Jackson State University	Jackson, Miss. 39217	7,718
Kentucky State University	Frankfort, Ky. 40601	2,246
Langston University	Langston, Okla. 73050	1,159
Lincoln University	Jefferson City, Mo. 65101	2,485

(Table C.2   continued)

Name	Location	Number of Students
University of Maryland (UMES)	Princess Anne, Md. 21853	1,034
Morgan State University	Baltimore, Md. 21239	4,583
Elizabeth City State University	Elizabeth City, N.C. 27909	1,605
Fayetteville State University	Fayetteville, N.C. 28301	2,002
North Carolina A&T State University	Greensboro, N.C. 27412	5,209
North Carolina Central University	Durham, N.C. 27707	4,729
Winston-Salem State University	Winston-Salem, N.C. 27102	2,323
Prairie View A&M University	Prairie View, Tex. 77445	5,236
Savannah State College	Savannah, Ga. 31404	2,504
South Carolina State College	Orangeburg, S.C. 29117	3,589
Southern University A&M	Baton Rouge, La. 70813	8,351
Tennessee State University	Nashville, Tenn. 37203	5,128
Texas Southern University	Houston, Tex. 77004	8,531
West Virginia State College	Institute, W. Va. 25112	3,955

Source: Information Please Almanac (New York, 1977).

APPENDIX D

TABLE D.1

Significance of Difference Between Black Administrators
Working at Black and White Land-Grant Institutions
of Higher Education Relating to Sex

		Type of Institution		
Sex	Count Row Pc t Col Pc t Total Pc t	Black 1	White 2	Row Total
Male	1.	137 60.9 74.1 44.5	88 39.1 71.5 28.6	225 73.1
Female	2.	48 57.8 25.9 15.6	35 42.2 28.5 11.4	83 26.9
Column total		185 60.1	123 39.9	308 100.0

Corrected chi-square = .12603 with 1 degree of freedom. Significance = .7226. Number of missing observations = 11.
Source: Compiled by the author.

TABLE D.2

Significance of Difference Between Black Administrators
Working at Black and White Land-Grant Institutions
of Higher Education Relating to Their
Highest Educational Level

Educational Level	Count Row Pc t Col Pc t Total Pc t	Type of Institution		Row Total
		Black 1	White 2	
No formal	1.	1 33.3 .5 .3	2 66.7 1.6 .6	3 1.0
B.S. or B.A.	3.	15 53.6 8.0 4.8	13 46.4 10.3 4.1	28 8.9
M.A. or M.S.	4.	61 60.4 32.4 19.4	40 39.6 31.7 12.7	101 32.2
Ed.S.	5.	0 .0 .0 .0	3 100.0 2.4 1.0	3 1.0

144

Educational Level	Count Row Pc t Col Pc t Total Pc t	Type of Institution		Row Total
		Black	White	
		1	2	
M.D., D.D.S., or J.D.	6.	4 44.4 2.1 1.3	5 56.6 4.0 1.6	9 2.9
Ed.D. or Ph.D.	7.	104 63.4 55.3 33.1	60 36.6 47.6 19.1	164 52.2
Other	8.	3 50.0 1.6 1.0	3 50.0 2.4 1.0	6 1.9
Column total		188 59.9	126 40.1	314 100.0

Chi-square = 7.82141 with 6 degrees of freedom. Significance = .2515. Number of missing observations = 5.

Source: Compiled by the author.

TABLE D.3

Significance of Difference Between Black Administrators
Working at Black and White Land-Grant Institutions
of Higher Education Relating to Where They Earned
Their Ph.D. (or Other Terminal Degree)

	Count	Type of Institution		Row Total
	Row Pc t	Black	White	
	Col Pc t			
Ph.D.	Total Pc t	1	2	
1. Predominantly white		108	69	177
		61.0	39.0	98.9
		98.2	100.0	
		60.3	38.5	
2. Predominantly black		2	0	2
		100.0	.0	1.1
		1.8	.0	
		1.1	.0	
Column total		110	69	179
		61.5	38.5	100.0

Corrected chi-square = .15671 with 1 degree of freedom. Significance = .6922. Number of missing observations = 140.

Source: Compiled by the author.

TABLE D.4

Significance of Difference Between Black Administrators
Working at Black and White Land-Grant Institutions
of Higher Education Relating to Fathers'
Highest Educational Level

| | Count | Type of Institution | | |
| | | Black | White | Row Total |
Fathers' Education	Row Pc t Col Pc t Total Pc t	1	2	
1. Less than high school		109 61.2 58.3 34.8	69 38.8 54.8 22.0	178 56.9
2. High school graduate		41 61.2 21.9 13.1	26 38.8 20.6 8.3	67 21.4
3. Associate degree		13 81.3 7.0 4.2	3 18.8 2.4 1.0	16 5.1
4. B.S. or B.A.		10 52.6 5.3 3.2	9 47.4 7.1 2.9	19 6.1
5. M.S. or M.A.		8 47.1 4.3 2.6	9 52.9 7.1 2.9	17 5.4

(continued)

		Type of Institution		Row Total
Fathers' Education	Count Row Pc t Col Pc t Total Pc t	Black 1	White 2	
Ed.S.		1 100.0 .5 .3	0 .0 .0 .0	1 5.4
M.D., D.D.S., or J.D.	7.	2 50.0 1.1 .6	2 50.0 1.6 .6	4 1.3
Ed.D. or Ph.D.	8.	1 100.0 .5 .3	0 .0 .0 .0	1 .3
Other	9.	2 20.0 1.1 .6	8 80.0 6.3 2.6	10 3.2
Column total		187 59.7	126 40.3	313 100.0

Chi-square = 12.91061 with 8 degrees of freedom. Significance = .1150. Number of missing observations = 6.

Source: Compiled by the author.

TABLE D.5

Significance of Difference Between Black Administrators
Working at Black and White Land-Grant Institutions
of Higher Education Relating to Mothers'
Highest Educational Level

Mothers' Education	Count Row Pc t Col Pc t Total Pc t	Type of Institution		Row Total
		Black	White	
		1	2	
No formal degree	1.	117 2.6 63.6 37.9	70 37.4 56.0 22.7	187 60.5
Associate degree	2.	13 56.5 7.1 4.2	10 43.5 8.0 3.2	23 7.4
B.S., B.A., or R.N.	3.	24 61.5 13.0 7.8	15 38.5 12.0 4.9	39 12.6

(continued)

(Table D.5   continued)

Mothers' Education	Count Row Pc t Col Pc t Total Pc t	Type of Institution		Row Total
		Black	White	
		1	2	
M.S. or M.A.	4.	5 50.0 2.7 1.6	5 50.0 4.0 1.6	10 3.2
Ed.S.	5.	1 100.0 .5 .3	0 .0 .0 .0	1 .3
Other	8.	24 49.0 13.0 7.8	25 51.0 20.0 8.1	49 15.9
Column total		184 59.5	125 40.5	309 100.0

Chi-square = 4.18881 with 5 degrees of freedom. Significance = .5226. Number of missing observations = 10.

Source: Compiled by the author.

TABLE D.6

Significance of Difference Between Black Administrators
Working at Black and White Land-Grant Institutions
of Higher Education Relating to
Fathers' Occupational Level

| Fathers' Occupation | Count Row Pc t Col Pc t Total Pc t | Type of Institution | | Row Total |
		Black 1	White 2	
Laborer	1.	61 63.5 32.6 19.6	35 36.5 28.0 11.2	96 30.8
Semiskilled	2.	30 58.8 16.0 9.6	21 41.2 16.8 6.7	51 16.3
Skilled	3.	27 54.0 14.4 8.7	23 46.0 18.4 7.4	50 16.0

(continued)

	Count	Type of Institution		Row Total
Fathers' Occupation	Row Pc t Col Pc t Total Pc t	Black 1	White 2	
Semiprofessional	4.	19 63.3 10.2 6.1	11 36.7 8.8 3.5	30 9.6
Professional	5.	28 51.9 15.0 9.0	26 48.1 20.8 8.3	54 17.3
Other	6.	22 71.0 11.8 7.1	9 29.0 7.2 2.9	31 9.9
Column total		187 59.9	125 40.1	312 100.0

Chi-square = 4.46472 with 5 degrees of freedom. Significance = .4846. Number of missing observations = 7.

Source: Compiled by the author.

TABLE D.7

Significance of Difference Between Black Administrators
Working at Black and White Land–Grant Institutions
of Higher Education Relating to
Mothers' Occupational Level

| Mothers' Occupation | Count Row Pc t Col Pc t Total Pc t | Type of Institution | | Row Total |
		Black 1	White 2	
Laborer	1.	76 62.8 41.8 24.8	45 37.2 36.0 14.7	121 39.4
Semiskilled	2.	17 53.1 9.3 5.5	15 46.9 12.0 4.9	32 10.4
Skilled	3.	5 29.4 2.7 1.6	12 70.6 9.6 3.9	17 5.5

(continued)

Mothers' Occupation	Count Row Pc t Col Pc t Total Pc t	Type of Institution		Row Total
		Black 1	White 2	
Semiprofessional	4.	19 54.3 10.4 6.2	16 45.7 12.8 5.2	35 11.4
Professional	5.	30 60.0 16.5 9.8	20 40.0 16.0 6.5	50 16.3
Other	6.	35 67.3 19.2 11.4	17 32.7 13.6 5.5	52 16.9
Column total		182 59.3	125 40.7	307 100.0

Chi-square = 9.17048 with 5 degrees of freedom. Significance = .1025. Number of missing observations = 12.

Source: Compiled by the author.

APPENDIX E

APPENDIX E

TABLE E.1

Significance of Difference Between Black Administrators
Working at Black and White Land-Grant Institutions of
Higher Education Relating to the Perceived Reasons
for Difficulty in Obtaining Present Position

		Type of Institution		Row Total
	Count Row Pc t Col Pc t			Row Total
		Black	White	Row Total
Due to	Total Pc t	1	2	
Job market requirements	1.	5 45.5 12.2 6.3	6 54.5 15.8 7.6	11 13.9
Own requirements	2.	5 50.0 12.2 6.3	5 50.0 13.2 6.3	10 12.7
Race	3.	0 .0 .0 .0	2 100.0 5.3 2.5	2 2.5

(continued)

Due to	Count Row Pc t Col Pc t Total Pc t	Type of Institution		Row Total
		Black 1	White 2	
Sex	4.	2 66.7 4.9 2.5	1 33.3 2.6 1.3	3 3.8
Institution from which graduated	5.	1 100.0 2.4 1.3	0 .0 .0 .0	1 1.3
Other	6.	28 53.8 68.3 35.4	24 46.2 63.2 30.4	52 65.8
Column total		41 51.9	38 48.1	79 100.0

Chi-square = 3.62324 with 5 degrees of freedom. Significance = .6048. Number of missing observations = 240.

Source: Compiled by the author.

TABLE E.2

Significance of Difference Between Black Administrators
Working at Black and White Land-Grant Institutions
of Higher Education Relating to the Type of
Position They Are Filling

New or Vacant	Count Row Pc t Col Pc t Total Pc t	Type of Institution		Row Total
		Black 1	White 2	
New position	1.	55 50.0 34.0 19.5	55 50.0 45.8 19.5	110 39.0
Vacancy	2.	106 62.4 65.4 37.6	64 37.6 53.3 22.7	170 60.3
Do not know	3.	1 50.0 .6 .4	1 50.0 .8 .4	1 .7
Column total		162 57.4	120 42.6	282 100.0

Chi-square = 4.21464 with 2 degrees of freedom. Significance = .1216. Number of missing observations = 37.

<u>Source:</u> Compiled by the author.

APPENDIX F

TABLE F.1

Significance of Difference Between Black Administrators
Working at Black and White Land-Grant Institutions
of Higher Education Relating to the
Type of Students They Teach

		Type of Institution		
	Count			Row Total
	Row Pc t	Black	White	
	Col Pc t			
Students	Total Pc t	1	2	
Undergraduate	1.	42 73.7 24.1 14.3	15 26.3 12.6 5.1	57 19.5
Graduate	2.	17 56.7 9.8 5.8	13 43.3 10.9 4.4	30 10.2
Graduate and undergraduate	3.	32 60.4 18.4 10.9	21 39.6 17.6 7.2	53 18.1
Do not teach	4.	83 54.2 47.7 28.3	70 45.8 58.8 23.9	153 52.2
Column total		174 59.4	119 40.6	293 100.0

Chi-square = 6.61941 with 3 degrees of freedom. Significance =
.0851. Number of missing observations = 26.
Source: Compiled by the author.

TABLE F.2

Significance of Difference Between Black Administrators
Working at Black and White Land-Grant Institutions
of Higher Education Relating to the Length
of Their Yearly Appointment

		Type of Institution		
	Count			Row Total
	Row Pc t	Black	White	
	Col Pc t			
Length of Appointment	Total Pc t	1	2	
Academic year	1.	21 77.8 11.4 6.9	6 22.2 5.0 2.0	27 8.9
Calendar year	2.	162 58.7 88.0 53.3	114 41.3 95.0 37.5	276 90.8
Other	3.	1 100.0 .5 .3	0 .0 .0 .0	1 .3
Column total		184 60.5	120 39.5	304 100.0

Chi-square = 4.40260 with 2 degrees of freedom. Significance =
.1107. Number of missing observations = 15.
Source: Compiled by the author.

TABLE F.3

Significance of Difference Between Black Administrators
Working at Black and White Land-Grant Institutions of
Higher Education Relating to Their Annual Salary

		Type of Institution		
		---	---	
	Count			
	Row Pc t	Black	White	Row Total
	Col Pc t			
Annual Salary	Total Pc t	1	2	
Less than $15,000	1.	14 46.7 7.5 4.5	16 53.3 12.9 5.2	30 9.7
$15,000– $17,499	2.	18 48.6 9.7 5.8	19 51.4 15.3 6.1	37 11.9
$17,500– $19,999	3.	23 59.0 12.4 7.4	16 41.0 12.9 5.2	39 12.6
$20,000– $22,499	4.	31 77.5 16.7 10.0	9 22.5 7.3 2.9	40 12.9
$22,500– $24,999	5.	30 63.8 16.1 9.7	17 36.2 13.7 5.5	47 15.2

(continued)

165

Annual Salary	Count Row Pc t Col Pc t Total Pc t	Type of Institution		Row Total
		Black 1	White 2	
$25,000-$29,999	6.	44 62.0 23.7 14.2	27 38.0 21.8 8.7	71 22.1
$30,000-$34,999	7.	18 66.7 9.7 5.8	9 33.3 7.3 2.9	27 8.7
$35,000 or above	8.	8 42.1 4.3 2.6	11 57.9 8.9 3.5	19 6.1
Column total		186 60.0	124 40.0	310 100.0

Chi-square = 12.76731 with 7 degrees of freedom. Significance = .0780. Number of missing observations = 9.

Source: Compiled by the author.

TABLE F.4

Significance of Difference Between Black Administrators
Working at Black and White Land-Grant Institutions of
Higher Education Relating to the Percentage of Time
Devoted to Research and Writing

| Research/ Writing | Count
Row Pc t
Col Pc t
Total Pc t | Type of Institution | | Row Total |
| | | Black | White | |
		1	2	
0-9	1.	104 61.5 68.1 34.3	65 38.5 52.4 21.5	169 55.8
10-19	2.	29 46.0 16.2 9.6	34 54.0 27.4 11.2	63 20.8
20-29	3.	19 61.3 10.6 6.3	12 38.7 9.7 4.0	31 10.2
30-39	4.	8 57.1 4.5 2.6	6 42.9 4.8 2.0	14 4.6
40-49	5.	2 33.3 1.1 .7	4 66.7 3.2 1.3	6 2.0

(continued)

Research/ Writing	Count Row Pc t Col Pc t Total Pc t	Black 1	White 2	Row Total
	Type of Institution			
50–59	6.	4 66.7 2.2 1.3	2 33.3 1.6 .7	6 2.0
60–69	7.	4 80.0 2.2 1.3	1 20.0 .8 .3	5 1.7
70–79	8.	3 100.0 1.7 1.0	0 .0 .0 .0	3 1.0
90–100	10.	6 100.0 3.4 2.0	0 .0 .0 .0	6 2.0
Column total		179 59.1	124 40.9	303 100.0

Chi-square = 13.87002 with 8 degrees of freedom. Significance = .0852. Number of missing observations = 16.
Source: Compiled by the author.

TABLE F.5

Significance of Difference Between Black Administrators
Working at Black and White Land-Grant Institutions
of Higher Education Relating to the Percentage of
Time Devoted to Administration

		Type of Institution		
	Count			Row Total
	Row Pc t	Black	White	
	Col Pc t			
Administration	Total Pc t	1	2	
0-9	1.	5 71.4 2.7 1.6	2 28.6 1.6 .6	7 2.3
10-19	2.	2 50.0 1.1 6	2 50.0 1.6 .6	4 1.3
20-29	3.	5 71.4 2.7 1.6	2 28.6 1.6 .6	7 2.3
30-39	4.	7 63.6 3.8 2.3	4 36.4 3.2 1.3	11 3.5
40-49	5.	17 65.4 9.2 5.5	9 34.6 7.2 2.9	26 8.4

(continued)

169

Administration	Count Row Pc t Col Pc t Total Pc t	Type of Institution		Row Total
		Black	White	
		1	2	
50-59	6.	19 65.5 10.3 6.1	10 34.5 8.0 3.2	29 9.4
60-69	7.	10 52.6 5.4 3.2	9 47.4 7.2 2.9	19 6.1
70-79	8.	16 43.2 8.6 5.2	21 56.8 16.8 6.8	37 11.9
80-89	9.	26 49.1 14.1 8.4	27 50.9 21.6 8.7	53 17.1
90-100	10.	78 66.7 42.2 25.2	39 33.3 31.2 12.6	117 37.7
Column total		185 59.7	125 40.3	310 100.0

Chi-square = 11.19801 with 9 degrees of freedom. Significance = .2624. Number of missing observations = 9.

Source: Compiled by the author.

TABLE F.6

Significance of Difference Between Black Administrators
Working at Black and White Land-Grant Institutions
of Higher Education Relating to the Origin
of the Funding for Their Positions

| | | Type of Institution | | |
		Black	White	Row Total
	Count			
	Row Pc t			
	Col Pc t			
Origin	Total Pc t	1	2	
Outside	1.	22	7	29
		75.9	24.1	9.4
		11.9	5.7	
		7.1	2.3	
Institution	2.	162	116	278
		58.3	41.7	90.3
		87.6	94.3	
		52.6	37.7	
Other	3.	1	0	1
		100.0	.0	.3
		.5	.0	
		.3	.0	
Column total		185	123	308
		60.1	39.9	100.0

Chi-square = 4.05388 with 2 degrees of freedom. Significance = .1317. Number of missing observations = 11.

Source: Compiled by the author.

TABLE F.7

Significance of Difference Between Black Administrators
Working at Black and White Land-Grant Institutions
of Higher Education Relating to the Type of
Fund Raising That Their Jobs Depend On

Job Depends On	Count Row Pc t Col Pc t Total Pc t	Black 1	White 2	Row Total
		Type of Institution		
1. Raise funds	1.	8 66.7 4.3 2.6	4 33.3 3.3 1.4	12 3.9
2. Institution raise funds	2.	3 42.9 1.6 1.0	4 57.1 3.3 1.3	2.3
3. Neither	3.	173 60.5 94.0 56.7	113 39.5 93.4 37.0	286 93.8
Column total		184 60.3	121 39.7	305 100.0

Chi-square = 1.09731 with 2 degrees of freedom. Significance =
.5777. Number of missing observations = 14.
Source: Compiled by the author.

TABLE F.8

Significance of Difference Between Black Administrators
Working at Black and White Land–Grant Institutions of
Higher Education Relating to the Number of Books
Written, Edited, Reviewed, or Co-Authored
in the Past Five Years

		Type of Institution		
		Black	White	Row Total
Count Row Pc t Col Pc t Total Pc t		1	2	
No. of Books:	1.	28 71.8 63.6 43.1	11 28.2 52.4 16.9	39 60.0
	2.	10 71.4 22.7 15.4	4 28.6 19.0 6.2	14 21.5
	3.	2 50.0 4.5 3.1	2 50.0 9.5 3.1	4 6.2
	4.	2 100.0 4.5 3.1	0 .0 .0 .0	2 3.1
	5.	1 50.0 2.3 1.5	1 50.0 4.8 1.5	2 3.1

(continued)

Count Row Pc t Col Pc t Total Pc t	Type of Institution		Row Total
	Black	White	
	1	2	
No. of Books: 6.	0	2	2
	.0	100.0	3.1
	.0	9.5	
	.0	3.1	
8.	1	0	1
	100.0	.0	1.5
	2.3	.0	
	1.5	.0	
15.	0	1	1
	.0	100.0	1.5
	.0	4.8	
	.0	1.5	
Column total	44	21	65
	67.7	32.3	100.0

Chi-square = 8.96581 with 7 degrees of freedom. Significance = .2551. Number of missing observations = 254.

Source: Compiled by the author.

TABLE F.9

Significance of Difference Between Black Administrators
Working at Black and White Land-Grant Institutions of
Higher Education Relating to the Number of Articles
Written, Edited, Reviewed, or Co-Authored
in the Past Five Years

Count Row Pc t Col Pc t Total Pc t	Type of Institution		Row Total
	Black	White	
	1	2	
No. of Articles: 1.	14 45.2 11.1 6.8	17 54.8 21.5 8.3	31 15.1
2.	24 58.5 19.0 11.7	17 41.5 21.5 8.3	41 20.0
3.	22 66.7 17.5 10.7	11 33.3 13.9 5.4	33 16.1
4.	11 64.7 15.1 9.3	6 35.3 15.2 5.9	17 8.3
5.	19 61.3 15.1 9.3	12 38.7 15.2 5.9	31 15.1
6.	9 81.8 7.1 4.4	2 18.2 2.5 1.0	11 5.4

(continued)

		Type of Institution		Row Total
Count Row Pc t Col Pc t Total Pc t		Black	White	
		1	2	
No. of Articles:	7.	4 80.0 3.2 2.0	1 20.0 1.3 .5	5 2.4
	8.	7 70.0 5.6 3.4	3 30.0 3.8 1.5	10 4.9
	9.	1 33.3 .8 .5	2 66.7 2.5 1.0	3 1.5
	10.	7 70.0 5.6 3.4	3 30.0 3.8 1.5	10 4.9
	11.	1 100.0 .8 .5	0 .0 .0 .0	1 .5

(Table F.9   continued)

	Count Row Pc t Col Pc t Total Pc t	Type of Institution		Row Total
		Black	White	
		1	2	
No. of Articles:	12.	1 50.0 .8 .5	1 50.0 1.3 .5	2 1.0
	13.	1 100.0 .8 .5	0 .0 .0 .0	1 .5
	15.	2 100.0 1.6 1.0	0 .0 .0 .0	2 1.0
	16.	0 .0 .0 .0	1 100.0 1.3 .5	1 .5
	20.	1 100.0 .8 .5	0 .0 .0 .0	1 .5

(continued)

Count Row Pc t Col Pc t Total Pc t	Type of Institution		Row Total
	Black	White	
	1	2	
No. of Articles: 30.	0 .0 .0 .0	1 100.0 1.3 .5	1 .5
31.	1 100.0 .8 .5	0 .0 .0 .0	1 .5
35.	0 .0 .0 .0	1 100.0 1.3 .5	1 .5
40.	1 100.0 .8 .5	0 .0 .0 .0	1 .5
54.	0 .0 .0 .0	1 100.0 1.3 .5	1 .5
Column total	126 61.5	79 38.5	205 100.0

Chi-square = 19.22622 with 20 degrees of freedom. Significance = .5072. Number of missing observations = 114.
    Source: Compiled by the author.

TABLE F.10

Significance of Difference Between Black Administrators
Working at Black and White Land-Grant Institutions of
Higher Education Relating to the Number of Theses
They Have Directed in the Past Five Years

		Type of Institution		
	Count	Black	White	Row Total
	Row Pc t			
	Col Pc t			
	Total Pc t	1	2	
No. of Theses:	1.	5	3	8
		62.5	37.5	17.0
		15.6	20.0	
		10.6	6.4	
	2.	7	4	11
		63.6	36.4	23.4
		21.9	26.7	
		14.9	8.5	
	3.	5	0	5
		100.0	.0	10.6
		15.6	.0	
		10.6	.0	
	4.	3	3	6
		50.0	50.0	12.8
		9.4	20.0	
		6.4	6.4	
	5.	1	2	3
		33.3	66.7	6.4
		3.1	13.3	
		2.1	4.3	

(continued)

	Count Row Pc t Col Pc t Total Pc t	Type of Institution		Row Total
		Black	White	
		1	2	
No. of Theses:	6.	3	0	3
		100.0	.0	6.4
		9.4	.0	
		6.4	.0	
	8.	1	0	1
		100.0	.0	2.1
		3.1	.0	
		2.1	.0	
	10.	2	1	3
		66.7	33.3	6.4
		6.3	6.7	
		4.3	2.1	
	13.	1	0	1
		100.0	.0	2.1
		3.1	.0	
		2.1	.0	
	15.	1	0	1
		100.0	.0	2.1
		3.1	.0	
		2.1	.0	
	16.	0	1	1
		.0	100.0	2.1
		.0	6.7	
		.0	2.1	

	Count	Type of Institution		Row Total
No. of Theses:	Row Pct	Black	White	
	Col Pct			
	Total Pct	1	2	
	20.	1 100.0 3.1 2.1	0 .0 .0 .0	1 2.1
	22.	0 .0 .0 .0	1 100.0 6.7 2.1	1 2.1
	23.	1 100.0 3.1 2.1	0 .0 .0 .0	1 2.1
	50.	1 100.0 3.1 2.1	2 .0 .0 .0	1 2.1
Column total		32 68.1	15 31.9	47 100.0

Chi-square = 13.61746 with 14 degrees of freedom. Significance = .4786. Number of missing observations = 272.

Source: Compiled by the author.

TABLE F.11

Significance of Difference Between Black Administrators
Working at Black and White Land-Grant Institutions
of Higher Education Relating to the Number
of Dissertations They Have Directed
in the Past Five Years

	Count	Type of Institution		Row Total
	Row Pc t	Black	White	
	Col Pc t			
	Total Pc t	1	2	
No. of Disserta-tions:	1.	0 .0 .0 .0	5 100.0 35.7 31.3	5 31.3
	2.	1 33.3 50.0 6.3	2 66.7 14.3 12.5	3 18.8
	3.	0 .0 .0 .0	3 100.0 21.4 18.8	3 18.8
	4.	0 .0 .0 .0	1 100.0 7.1 6.3	1 6.3

(Table F.11   continued)

	Count Row Pc t Col Pc t Total Pc t	Type of Institution		Row Total
		Black 1	White 2	
No. of Dissertations:	6.	1 50.0 50.0 6.3	1 50.0 7.1 6.3	2 12.5
	7.	0 .0 .0 .0	1 100.0 7.1 6.3	1 6.3
	8.	0 .0 .0 .0	1 100.0 7.1 6.3	1 6.3
Column total		2 12.5	14 87.5	16 100.0

Chi-square = 5.33333 with 6 degrees of freedom. Significance = .5018. Number of missing observations = 303.

Source: Compiled by the author.

TABLE F.12

Significance of Difference Between Black Administrators
Working at Black and White Land-Grant Institutions
of Higher Education Relating to the Number of
Thesis Committees They Have Served On

		Type of Institution		
	Count			
	Row Pc t	Black	White	Row Total
	Col Pc t			
	Total Pc t	1	2	
No. of Thesis Committees:	1.	5 55.6 11.4 7.0	4 44.4 14.8 5.6	9 12.7
	2.	7 77.8 15.9 9.9	2 22.2 7.4 2.8	9 12.7
	3.	4 50.0 9.1 5.6	4 50.0 14.8 5.6	8 11.3
	4.	1 50.0 2.3 1.4	1 50.0 3.7 1.4	2 2.8
	5.	4 80.0 9.1 5.6	1 20.0 3.7 1.4	5 7.0
	6.	4 57.1 9.1 5.6	3 42.9 11.1 4.2	7 9.9

	Count	Type of Institution		
	Row Pc t	Black	White	Row Total
	Col Pc t			
	Total Pc t	1	2	
No. of Thesis Committees:	7.	4 57.1 9.1 5.6	3 42.9 11.1 4.2	7 9.9
	8.	1 50.0 2.3 1.4	1 50.0 3.7 1.4	2 2.8
	10.	4 100.0 9.1 5.6	0 .0 .0 .0	4 5.6
	12.	1 50.0 2.3 1.4	1 50.0 3.7 1.4	2 2.8
	15.	2 66.7 4.5 2.8	1 33.3 3.7 1.4	3 4.2
	16.	1 100.0 2.3 1.4	0 .0 .0 .0	1 1.4

(continued)

	Count	Type of Institution		Row Total
	Row Pc t	Black	White	
	Col Pc t			
	Total Pc t	1	2	
No. of Thesis Committees:	19.	0 .0 .0 .0	2 100.0 7.4 2.8	2 2.8
	25.	1 50.0 2.3 1.4	1 50.0 3.7 1.4	2 2.8
	30.	1 50.0 2.3 1.4	1 50.0 3.7 1.4	2 2.8
	36.	0 .0 .0 .0	1 100.0 3.7 1.4	1 1.4
	40.	1 100.0 2.3 1.4	0 .0 .0 .0	1 1.4

	Count Row Pc t Col Pc t Total Pc t	Type of Institution		Row Total
		Black	White	
		1	2	
No. of Thesis Committees:	50.	2 100.0 4.5 2.8	0 .0 .0 .0	2 2.8
	60.	1 100.0 2.3 1.4	0 .0 .0 .0	1 1.4
	80.	0 .0 .0 .0	1 100.0 3.7 1.4	1 1.4
Column total		44 62.0	27 38.0	71 100.0

Chi-square = 15.10339 with 19 degrees of freedom. Significance = .7160. Number of missing observations = 248.
  Source: Compiled by the author.

TABLE F.13

Significance of Difference Between Black Administrators
Working at Black and White Land-Grant Institutions
of Higher Education Relating to the Number of
Dissertation Committees They Have Served On

		Type of Institution		
	Count	Black	White	Row Total
	Row Pc t			
	Col Pc t			
	Total Pc t	1	2	
No. of Disserta-tion Committees:	1.	6 66.7 50.0 16.2	3 33.3 12.0 8.1	9 24.3
	2.	1 16.7 8.3 2.7	5 83.3 20.0 13.5	6 16.2
	3.	3 60.0 25.0 8.1	2 40.0 8.0 5.4	5 13.5
	4.	1 100.0 8.3 2.7	0 .0 .0 .0	1 2.7
	5.	0 .0 .0 .0	4 100.0 16.0 10.8	4 10.8

	Type of Institution		
Count			Row Total
Row Pct	Black	White	
Col Pc t			
Total Pc t	1	2	
No. of Disserta- tion Committees: 6.	0 .0 .0 .0	2 100.0 8.0 5.4	2 5.4
7.	1 33.3 8.3 2.7	2 66.7 8.0 5.4	3 8.1
10.	0 .0 .0 .0	1 100.0 4.0 2.7	1 2.7
12.	0 .0 .0 .0	1 100.0 4.0 2.7	1 2.7
15.	0 .0 .0 .0	2 100.0 8.0 5.4	2 5.4

(continued)

		Type of Institution		
	Count			Row Total
	Row Pc t	Black	White	
	Col Pc t			
	Total Pc t	1	2	
No. of Disserta-tion Committees:	18.	0 .0 .0 .0	1 100.0 4.0 2.7	1 2.7
	21.	0 .0 .0 .0	1 100.0 4.0 2.7	1 2.7
	25.	0 .0 .0 .0	1 100.0 4.0 2.7	1 2.7
Column total		12 32.4	25 67.6	37 100.0

Chi-square = 15.55233 with 12 degrees of freedom. Significance = .2126. Number of missing observations = 282.

Source: Compiled by the author.

APPENDIX G

TABLE G.1

Significance of Difference Between Black Administrators
Working at Black and White Land-Grant Institutions
of Higher Education Relating to Their Being
Full-Time or Part-Time Administrators

Count Row Pc t Col Pc t Total Pc t	Type of Institution		Row Total
	Black	White	
	1	2	
Full time 1.	149 57.8 82.8 49.5	109 42.2 90.1 36.2	258 85.7
Part time 2.	31 72.1 17.2 10.3	12 27.9 9.9 4.0	43 14.3
Column total	180 59.8	121 40.2	301 100.0

Corrected chi-square = 2.58492 with 1 degree of freedom.
Significance = .1019. Number of missing observations = 18.
Source: Compiled by the author.

TABLE G.2

Significance of Difference Between Black Administrators
Working at Black and White Land-Grant Institutions
of Higher Education Relating to Their Authority

	Count Row Pc t Col Pc t	Type of Institution		
Authority	Total Pc t	Black 1	White 2	Row Total
Department	1.	43 67.2 28.3 18.8	21 32.8 27.3 9.2	64 27.9
College	2.	58 75.3 38.2 25.3	19 24.7 24.7 8.3	77 33.6
Institution	3.	22 62.9 14.5 9.6	13 37.1 16.9 5.7	35 15.3
Other	4.	29 54.7 19.1 12.7	24 45.3 31.2 10.5	53 23.1
Column total		152 66.4	77 33.6	229 100.0

Chi-square = 6.20386 with 3 degrees of freedom. Significance =
.1021. Number of missing observations=90.
Source: Compiled by the author.

TABLE G.3[*]

Percentage Breakdown of Authority Over Other Academic
and Administrative Positions for Black Administrators
Working at Black and White Land-Grant Institutions

Academic Authority	Count Row Pc t Col Pc t Total Pc t	Type of Institution		Row Total
		Black 1	White 2	
	1.	86 60.6 100.0 60.6	56 39.4 100.0 39.4	142 100.0
Column total		86 60.6	56 39.4	142 100.0

Number of missing observations = 177.
*Supplement to Table G.2.
Source: Compiled by the author.

TABLE G.4[*]

Percentage Breakdown of Authority Over Classified Staff
for Black Administrators Working at Black and White
Land-Grant Institutions

		Type of Institution		
	Count			
	Row Pc t	Black	White	Row Total
	Col Pc t			
Classified	Total Pc t	1	2	
	2.	113	75	188
		60.1	39.9	100.0
		100.0	100.0	
		60.1	39.9	
Column total		113	75	188
		60.1	39.9	100.0

Number of missing observations = 131.
[*]Supplement to Table G.2.
Source: Compiled by the author.

TABLE G.5[*]

Percentage Breakdown of Authority Over Fiscal Matters
for Black Administrators Working at Black and White
Land-Grant Institutions

	Count	Type of Institution		Row Total
	Row Pc t	Black	White	
	Col Pc t			
Fiscal	Total Pc t	1	2	
	3.	140	83	223
		62.8	37.2	100.0
		100.0	100.0	
		62.8	37.2	
Column total		140	83	223
		62.8	37.2	100.0

Number of missing observations = 96.
[*]Supplement to Table G.2.
Source: Compiled by the author.

TABLE G.6[*]

Percentage Breakdown of Authority Over Travel Within and Without State for Black Administrators Working at Black and White Land-Grant Institutions

		Type of Institution		
	Count	Black	White	Row Total
	Row Pc t			
	Col Pc t			
Travel	Total Pc t	1	2	
	4.	137	77	214
		64.0	36.0	100.0
		100.0	100.0	
		64.0	36.0	
Column total		137	77	214
		64.0	36.0	100.0

Number of missing observations = 105.
[*]Supplement to Table G.2.
Source: Compiled by the author.

TABLE G.7[*]

Percentage Breakdown of Authority Over Purchase of
Capital Equipment for Black Administrators Working
at Black and White Land-Grant Institutions

| | | Type of Institution | | |
		Black	White	Row Total
Purchase	Count Row Pc t Col Pc t Total Pc t	1	2	
	5.	109 65.7 100.0 65.7	57 34.3 100.0 34.3	166 100.0
Column total		109 65.7	57 34.3	166 100.0

Number of missing observations = 153.
[*]Supplement to Table G.2.
Source: Compiled by the author.

TABLE G.8

Significance of Difference Between Black Administrators
Working at Black and White Land-Grant Institutions of
Higher Education Relating to the Percentage of Their
Decisions That Are Rejected by Their Superiors

		Type of Institution		
	Count			Row Total
	Row Pc t	Black	White	
	Col Pc t			
Decisions	Total Pc t	1	2	
0-5	1.	128 61.0 74.0 44.0	82 39.0 69.5 28.2	210 72.2
6-10	2.	28 60.9 16.2 9.6	18 39.1 15.3 6.2	46 15.8
11-15	3.	6 60.0 3.5 2.1	4 40.0 3.4 1.4	10 3.4
16-20	4.	5 41.7 2.9 1.7	7 58.3 5.9 2.4	12 4.1

	Count	Type of Institution		Row Total
	Row Pc t	Black	White	
	Col Pc t			
Decisions	Total Pc t	1	2	
21–25	5.	1 25.0 .6 .3	3 75.0 2.5 1.0	4 1.4
26–30	6.	5 55.6 2.9 1.7	4 44.4 3.4 1.4	9 3.1
Column total		173 59.5	118 40.5	291 100.0

Chi square = 3.83640 with 5 degrees of freedom. Significance = .5732. Number of missing observations = 28.

Source: Compiled by the author.

TABLE G.9

Significance of Difference Between Black Administrators
Working at Black and White Land-Grant Institutions of
Higher Education Relating to How Their Decisions
Are Carried Out by Classified Staff

Decisions Carried Out	Count Row Pc t Col Pc t Total Pc t	Type of Institution		Row Total
		Black 1	White 2	
1. Readily	1.	147 61.5 83.5 50.7	92 38.5 80.7 31.7	239 82.4
2. Some hesitation	2.	24 66.7 13.6 8.3	12 33.3 10.5 4.1	36 12.4
3. Partially	3.	3 42.9 1.7 1.0	4 57.1 3.5 1.4	7 2.4
4. Other	4.	2 25.0 1.1 .7	6 75.0 5.3 2.1	8 2.8
Column total		176 60.7	114 39.3	290 100.0

Chi-square = 5.81016 with 3 degrees of freedom. Significance = .1212. Number of missing observations = 29.
Source: Compiled by the author.

BIBLIOGRAPHY

BOOKS

Green, Harry Washington, 1974. Holders of Doctorates Among American Negroes. Newton, Mass.: Crofton.

Isaac, Stephen, and Michael, B. 1971. Handbook in Research and Evaluation. San Diego: Robert Knapp.

Jencks, Christopher. 1972. Inequality. New York: Harper & Row.

Johnson, Roosevelt. 1974. Black Scholars on Higher Education in the 70s. Columbus, Ohio: ECCA Publications.

Kerlinger, Fred N. 1973. Foundations of Behavioral Research. New York: Holt, Rinehart and Winston.

Lassey, William R. 1971. Leadership and Social Change. Iowa City, Iowa: University Associates.

Moore, William, Jr., and Wagstaff, Lonnie H. 1974. Black Educators in White Colleges. San Francisco: Jossey-Bass.

Senter, R. J. 1969. Analysis of Data. Glenview, Ill.: Scott, Foresman.

Sergiovanni, Thomas J., and Carver, Fred D. 1973. The New School Executive. New York: Dodd, Mead.

Watson, Bernard C. 1972. The Black Administrator in Higher Education: Current Dilemmas, Problems and Opportunities. Philadelphia: Temple University Press.

ARTICLES

Blake, Elias, Jr. 1971. "Future Leadership Roles for Predominantly Black Colleges and Universities in American Higher Education." Daedalus 100, no. 3: 745-71.

Brown, J. C., et al. 1959. "Southern Negro and White Educators:
    A Comparison of Pertinent Characteristics." Journal of Negro
    Education 40 (Spring): 159-62.

Campbell, Roald F. 1959. "Educational Administration: Is It
    Unique?" School Review 67, no. 4 (Winter): 461-68.

Chiaravalloti, Joseph James. 1973. "Some Dynamics of Change in
    Personality and Value Orientation in a Biracial Training Pro-
    gram for School Administrators." Dissertation Abstracts
    International 34 (1-A) (July): 83.

Doddy, Hurley H. 1963. "The Progress of the Negro in Higher
    Education." Journal of Negro Education 32 (Fall): 485-92.

HoHauser, Harvey Ronald. 1972. "Comparative Attitudes Among
    College Administrators." Dissertation Abstracts International
    32 (9-A) (March): 4878.

Jackson, Jacquelyne J. 1970. "Black Ph.D.'s Reply." Transaction
    7 (October): 60.

Jencks, Christopher, and Riesman, David. 1967. "American Negro
    Colleges; Future of the Negro Colleges." Harvard Educational
    Review 37 (Winter): 43-60.

Johnson, R. 1969. "Black Administrators and Higher Education."
    Black Scholar 1 (November): 66-76.

Lyons, J. E. 1974. "Black Public Colleges: To Stay Open or to
    Close?" Integrated Education 12 (July): 22-23.

Mommsen, K. G. 1974. "Black Ph.D. in the Academic Market
    Place: Supply and Demand and Price." Journal of Higher
    Education 45 (April): 253-67.

Morris, E. W. 1972. "The Contemporary Negro College and the
    Brain Drain." Journal of Negro Education 41 (Fall): 39-319.

Parker, Franklin. 1961. "Negro Education in the U.S.A.: A Par-
    tial Bibliography of Doctoral Dissertations." Negro History
    Bulletin (May): 190-91.

Parker, J. E. 1963. "Assessment of the Attitudinal Climate for
    New Instructional Media Among Negro College Administrators."
    Negro Educational Review 14 (July-August): 146-54.

Pifer, A. 1974. "What Future for Black Public Colleges?" Compact
    8, no. 5 (Fall): 8.

Poinsett, A. 1970. "Dr. Charles G. Hurst: Master Mind of Mal-
    colm X College." Ebony, March, pp. 29-32.

Rafky, D. M. 1972. "Attitudes of Black Scholars Toward Black
    Colleges." Journal of Negro Education (Fall): 320-30.

Rose, H. M. 1966. "Appraisal of the Negro Educators' Situation in
    the Academic Market Place." Journal of Negro Education 35
    (Winter): 18-26.

Sawyer, B. E. 1963. "Graduate Training of Twenty-One Selected
    College Faculties." Journal of Negro Education 32 (Spring):
    193-97.

Shiver, W. B., Jr. 1973. "Black Professors: Salary or Service."
    Integrated Education 11 (July): 56-57.

Whiting, N. 1972. "Apartheid in American Higher Education."
    Educational Record 53 (Spring): 128-31.

Wiley, Bennie L. 1971. "A Different Breed of Administrator."
    Phi Delta Kappan 52 (Spring): 55.

Wolf, R. 1974. "Selected Differences Between Predominantly White
    and Predominantly Negro Schools in the U.S." Comparative
    Education Review 18 (June): 305-13.

"Black Ph.D.'s." 1970. Transaction 7 (May): 14.

"Blacks in Higher Education." 1976. Intellect 104 (April): 104.

"Casualties of Progress." 1971. Saturday Review, January, p. 53.

"Cheek Brothers: A New Breed of College President." 1969. Ebony,
    October, pp. 35-38.

"College Presidents and Minority Students." 1974. Integrated Education 12 (January): 41-44.

"Elusive Black Educator: How to Find, Hire and Keep Him." 1969. School Management 13 (March): 54-60.

"More Black Colleges Needed in the Right Places." 1972. Jet, February, p. 14.

"Negro in Administration." 1961. Overview 2 (June): 35-37.

"New Black Presidents." 1968. Time, December 27, pp. 48-49.

"Plight of Negro College Presidents." 1960. Ebony, October, pp. 138-40.

"The Progress of the Negro in Higher Education." 1963. Journal of Negro Education 32 (Fall): 485-92.

"Special Project for Developing Institutions." 1972. AAUP Bulletin 58 (June): 166-67.

"White Colleges and Negro Higher Education." 1967. Journal of Negro Education 36 (Summer): 258-65.

ABOUT THE AUTHOR

ROBERT L. HOSKINS received his B.A. from Dominican College in Racine, Wisconsin and his M.S. and Ph.D. from the University of Wisconsin-Milwaukee. Dr. Hoskins worked as an hourly factory employee before pursuing a college education. He was Coordinator of a Federal Anti-Poverty Program, and has been an Associate Dean of Student Affairs at the University of Wisconsin-Superior.

RELATED TITLES
Published by Praeger Special Studies

THE TWO-YEAR COLLEGE
INSTRUCTOR TODAY

Arthur M. Cohen
Florence B. Brawer

MINORITIES IN U.S. INSTITUTIONS OF
HIGHER EDUCATION

Frank Brown
Madelon D. Stent

SEX DISCRIMINATION IN CAREER
COUNSELING AND EDUCATION

Michele Harway
Helen S. Astin

FOREIGN STUDENTS IN THE UNITED STATES:
Coping Behavior Within the Educational Environment

W. Frank Hull, IV